INSTRUCTOR'S MANUAL

to Accompany

PSYCHOLINGUISTICS

edited by Jean Berko Gleason and Nan Bernstein Ratner

Instructor's Manual
prepared by
Pamela Gleason

Harcourt Brace Jovanovich College Publishers
Fort Worth Philadelphia San Diego New York Orlando Austin San Antonio
Toronto Montreal London Sydney Tokyo

ISBN: 0-03-055967-7

Copyright © 1993 by Harcourt Brace & Company.

All rights reserved. No part of this publication may be reproduced or transmitted in any form or by any means, electronic or mechanical, including photocopy, recording, or any information storage and retrieval system, without permission in writing from the publisher.

Permission is hereby granted to reproduce the Transparency Masters in this publication in complete pages, with the copyright notice, for instructional use and not for resale, by any teacher using classroom quantities of the related student textbook.

Address Editorial Correspondence To: Harcourt Brace Jovanovich, Inc.
301 Commerce Street, Suite 3700
Fort Worth Texas 76102

Address Orders To: Harcourt Brace Jovanovich, Inc.
6277 Sea Harbor Drive
Orlando Florida 32887
1-800-782-4479, or 1-800-433-0001 (in Florida)

Printed in the United States of America.

3 4 5 6 7 8 9 0 1 2   018   9 8 7 6 5 4 3 2 1

PREFACE

This manual is designed to accompany *Psycholinguistics*. For each chapter of the text, we have provided (1) a chapter outline; (2) a summary of the key concepts in the chapter; (3) multiple choice questions; (4) short answer questions; and (5) suggested topics for essay questions.

The Appendix contains exercises and instructional activities that we hope will demonstrate important material in the text and help to give students a real feeling for how psycholinguistic research is conducted. Please note that the appendix and ancillary demonstration tape contain material relevant to a number of different chapters. We suggest that the instructor read through the appendix initially while preparing the course syllabus, so that any equipment required for class demonstrations can be available.

The chapter outline and summary together provide a framework on which the instructor may build class lectures, or from which points of particular importance may be extracted. The instructional activities chosen by the instructor can then be selected and tailored to the size of the class and the level of the students. Many of the suggested short answer questions and essay questions can also be used as topics for class discussion or as starting points for student papers or projects.

One of the most burdensome tasks that faces any instructor is the creation of appropriate instruments for assessing student understanding. We have included a generous sampling of multiple choice questions here for each chapter, because, of all question types, they are the most time consuming to devise. To be even more useful to instructors, we have included as well a variety of short answer and essay questions.

Our thanks to the authors of the text chapters for their contributions to this manual, and to Dr. Harold Goodglass for allowing us to use his taped interviews with patients with aphasia, as well as to Dr. Jacqueline Sachs for the use of her experimental stimuli.

                                      Pamela Gleason
                                      Jean Berko Gleason
                                      Nan Bernstein Ratner
                                      January, 1993

CONTENTS

PREFACE — iii

CHAPTER ONE: AN INTRODUCTION TO PSYCHOLINGUISTICS
- Chapter Outline — 1
- Key Concepts — 1
- Multiple Choice Questions — 3
- Short Answer Questions — 6
- Essay Questions — 6

CHAPTER TWO: THE NEUROLOGICAL BASES OF HUMAN COMMUNICATION
- Chapter Outline — 7
- Key Concepts — 7
- Multiple Choice Questions — 10
- Short Answer Questions — 13
- Essay Questions — 14

CHAPTER THREE: SPEECH PERCEPTION
- Chapter Outline — 15
- Key Concepts — 15
- Multiple Choice Questions — 19
- Short Answer Questions — 22
- Essay Questions — 22

CHAPTER FOUR: WORDS AND MEANING
- Chapter Outline — 23
- Key Concepts — 24
- Multiple Choice Questions — 27
- Short Answer Questions — 30
- Essay Questions — 31

CHAPTER FIVE: SENTENCE PROCESSING
- Chapter Outline — 32
- Key Concepts — 32
- Multiple Choice Questions — 34
- Short Answer Questions — 37
- Essay Questions — 38

CHAPTER SIX: CONVERSATIONAL DISCOURSE
- Chapter Outline — 39
- Key Concepts — 39
- Multiple Choice Question — 42
- Short Answer Questions — 44
- Essay Questions — 45

CHAPTER SEVEN: SPEECH PRODUCTION
    Chapter Outline   46
    Key Concepts   46
    Multiple Choice Questions   49
    Short Answer Questions   52
    Essay Questions   52

CHAPTER EIGHT: LANGUAGE DEVELOPMENT IN CHILDREN
    Chapter Outline   53
    Key Concepts   54
    Multiple Choice Questions   58
    Short Answer Questions   60
    Essay Questions   61

CHAPTER NINE: A PSYCHOLINGUISTIC ACCOUNT OF READING
    Chapter Outline   62
    Key Concepts   62
    Multiple Choice Questions   66
    Short Answer Questions   69
    Essay Questions   70

CHAPTER TEN: BILINGUALISM AND SECOND LANGUAGE ACQUISITION
    Chapter Outline   71
    Key Concepts   71
    Multiple Choice Questions   74
    Short Answer Questions   77
    Essay Questions   78

APPENDIX   79

CHAPTER ONE: AN INTRODUCTION TO PSYCHOLINGUISTICS: *WHAT DO LANGUAGE USERS KNOW?*

CHAPTER OUTLINE

INTRODUCTION
WHAT IS PSYCHOLINGUISTICS?
    The domain of psycholinguistic inquiry
Language
    What is language?
Is language species specific?
    Distinguishing between language and speech
WHAT SPEAKERS AND LISTENERS KNOW: A BRIEF SURVEY OF LINGUISTICS
    Levels of language analysis
        Phonology
        Sequences of sounds (phonotactics)
        The lexicon
        Morphology: the study of word formation
        Syntax: combining words to form meaningful propositions
            Grammars
            Syntactic theory in the 60s: Transformational grammars
            Changes in grammatical theory
        Discourse and the pragmatics of language usage
        Metalinguistic capacity: the ability to analyze our own language competence
LANGUAGE DIVERSITY AND UNIVERSALS
    Oral and signed languages
    Written language
THE EVOLUTION OF PSYCHOLINGUISTIC INQUIRY
THE ACQUISITION OF LANGUAGE BY CHILDREN
SUMMARY

KEY CONCEPTS TO EMPHASIZE

A. Language is one of the most basic elements of human existence. The goal of psycholinguistics is to explore and understand the processes that underlie our ability to produce, comprehend and acquire language.

B. Language can be defined as a communication system that is rule governed, symbolic, hierarchically structured and infinitely creative. This means that the words and sounds that make up an utterance can be recombined following grammatical rules to convey an infinite variety of meanings. It also means that we can use language to discuss displaced or absent concepts, such as the meaning of freedom, or our opinions of political candidates.

C. Although many species of animal have fairly complex communication systems, and some primates have been able to learn sign language, language is species specific. Animal communication remains context dependent and animals are unable to produce the infinite variety of messages that characterize true language. Thus, language is a uniquely human behavior.

D. Although most languages in the world are spoken languages, language is not the same as speech. A number of languages are signed or gestural, and these languages embody all of the basic linguistic features of spoken languages. Users of sign languages, such as **American Sign Language (ASL)** have been shown to process language in ways very similar to users of spoken language. Thus, brain damage impairs spoken and signed communication in very similar ways, and signed errors ("slips of the hand") are very similar to spoken errors ("slips of the tongue").

E. Language understanding and production are dependent upon a number of smaller tasks. These are:
1. recognizing or being able to produce the sounds of the message
2. identifying or producing the words in the message and associating them with their meanings
3. analyzing or producing the grammatical structure of the message
4. evaluating the message in its current context or fitting the message to the context

F. The first task depends upon **phonology.** Phonology requires that the speaker or hearer understand the phonemic inventory of the language and is able to recognize and differentiate between different phonemes. The phonetic inventory of one language may be quite different from that of another. Successful use of a language also depends upon an understanding of **phonotactics**, i.e. the rules for combining different sounds into words.

G. The second task requires a familiarity with the **lexicon**. The lexicon can be considered a "mental dictionary" of words. Successful language production and comprehension also requires an understand of **morphology**, i.e. how words are formed.

H. The rules for combining words into grammatical sentences depends upon **syntax**. English syntax is often highly dependent upon word order. Because the typical word order in English is subject-verb-object, English is sometimes called an S-V-O language.

I. The study of syntax has been a major focus of linguistic inquiry as researchers attempt to come up with grammatical rules for well formed utterances. During the 1950s, linguist Noam Chomsky developed the theory of **Transformational Generative (TG) Grammar**, which is now known as the **Standard Theory**.

J. The Standard Theory distinguishes between **deep structures** and **surface structures**. The deep structure of a sentence is its underlying concept; the surface structure is the final grammatical expression of the underlying concept. Deep structures and surface structures can be derived from each other through transformations. Complex sentences are considered to be derived from several deep structures. The hypothesis known as the **Derivational Theory of Complexity (DTC)** arises from this concept.

K. The DTC hypothesis has been unable to explain grammatical competence fully. Over the years, several other theories of syntax have arisen. **Government and Binding (GB)** theory posits that the lexicon has a much greater role in the production of syntax. According to GB theory, words in the lexicon are already associated with a number of rules governing their appropriate use in sentences.

L. The successful expression or interpretation of a message finally rests upon **pragmatics**, i.e. the appropriate wording and interpretation of language in a social context. Pragmatics requires that a speaker understand her audience and tailor the message accordingly. Linguistic conventions about how to express oneself to different audiences are known as **registers**.

M. The minimal unit of a written language system is called a **grapheme**. Systems, such as English, whose graphemes represent phonemes, are called **alphabetic**. Other systems include **syllabaries**, in which the graphemes represent syllables, as well as systems that are not sound based, such as those that use **logograms** (symbols that represent whole words) or **ideograms** (symbols that represent ideas).

N. Although philosophers and scientists have been intrigued by the processes of language acquisition and production since the time of the ancient Greeks, the field of psycholinguistics came into being during the early 1950s. Early psycholinguistic theories were largely based upon behaviorist principles while many later theories were guided by Chomsky's Transformational Generative Grammar. The field of psycholinguistics is still evolving.

O. The study of language acquisition by children is an active area of psycholinguistic inquiry. Scholars are divided as to how much of language learning can be accounted for by the role of the environment, and how much is innate.

MULTIPLE CHOICE QUESTIONS

1. The field of psycholinguistics is concerned primarily with
    a. the psychological problems that underlie linguistic errors
 * b. the processes of language comprehension, language production and language acquisition.
    c. the psychological, anatomical and physiological basis of linguistic ability
    d. the ability to express and comprehend psychological problems
                                                                                  (PAGES 3-4)
2. When we say that language is species specific, we mean that
    a. different species of animals each have their own specific languages
 * b. only humans use a true language system
    c. animals can only use language to convey meanings that are specific to their own species.
    d. virtually all human beings spontaneously acquire a language
                                                                                  (PAGES 9-10)
3. The smallest sound recognized by speakers in a given language is known as a
 * a. phoneme
    b. morpheme
    c. lexicon
    d. affix
                                                                                  (PAGE 12)

4. Metalinguistics
    a. is the study of the rules of word formation and interpretation
 * b. refers to our ability to analyze and think about language
    c. is the study of the interrelationship between speech and psychological processes
    d. is a theory advanced by Skinner in the late 1950s, postulating that language can be learned by stimulus and response.

(PAGE 26)

5. When we say that a word is *multimorphemic* we mean that it
    a. is a word which can be interpreted in two or more ways
    b. can be added to by using suffixes and prefixes
    c. has several variant pronunciations
 * d. is divisible into two or more meaningful parts

(PAGE 19)

6. English is sometimes called an S-V-O language because
    a. it is simple, variable and objective
 * b. its usual word order in sentences is subject, verb, object
    c. its principal parts are subjects, verbs and objects
    d. it has syntax, verbs and orthography

(PAGE 21)

7. A written symbol that represents a word is called
    a. an ideogram
    b. a grapheme
    c. a syllabary
 * d. a logogram

(PAGE 32)

8. Transformational generative (TG) grammar is
 * a. a grammatical description of the rules of English developed by linguist Noam Chomsky in the 1950s.
    b. one of the characteristics of true language
    c. the process by which children learn the rules of pluralization
    d. the stage of language learning in which children begin to use the correct verb forms

(PAGE 23)

9. The smallest unit of meaning in a language is called a
    a. phoneme
    b. grapheme
 * c. morpheme
    d. syntactic structure

(PAGE 18)

10. Understanding rules for the permissible sequences of sounds in a language requires
 * a. phonotactics
    b. phonetic logic
    c. phonology
    d. phonics

(PAGE 16)

11. A parent's statement, *Your room is a mess,* is best viewed as:
    a. a deferential remark

-4-

      b. a direct order
      c. an ambiguous comment
*   d. an indirect order

(PAGE 25)

12. When a word or sentence is ambiguous,
      a. it cannot be understood by the listener
*   b. it is capable of more than one interpretation
      c. it is pragmatically inappropriate
      d. it is less frequent in the language

(PAGE 18)

13. The many pronunciation variants of a phoneme are called its:
      a. morphemes
*   b. allophones
      c. features
      d. phonathons

(PAGE 15)

14. The word *unties* contains:
*   a. one free and two bound morphemes
      b. two free morphemes
      c. three allomorphs
      d. three allophones

(PAGES 18-20)

15. A universal grammar is
      a. a set of rules children are all taught in grammar school
      b. a set of basic expressions which exist in all languages
*   c. a system of principles and rules that are elements of all true languages
      d. a hypothetical model of language learning which explains how children are able to generate the grammatical rules of their language

(PAGES 28-29)

16. Which of the following sentence types does **not** violate the usual word order of English sentences?
      a. passives
      b. datives
      c. center embedded relative clauses
*   d. simple active declaratives

(PAGES 20-22)

17. Phoneme-grapheme correspondences are:
*   a. rules for mapping sounds onto spelling
      b. rules for mapping sounds onto the lexicon
      c. rules for interpreting allophones
      d. rules for assigning the prosody of an utterance

(PAGE 32)

18. The mental lexicon is:
      a. a system of rules for generating well-formed sentences
      b. the neurological substrate underlying language use
*   c. a dictionary containing information regarding the meaning and grammatically appropriate use of words
      d. a system of rules for sequencing the sounds of a language

(PAGE 17)

19. The [p] in pot and the [p] in spot
    a. differ from one another in voicing
    b. are produced in identical ways
*   c. differ from one another because the first is aspirated, while the second is not
    d. differ from one another because one contains a meaningful contrast while the other does not

(PAGES 13 & 15)

20. The premise which underlies Reaction Time studies in psycholinguistics is:
*   a. that the time required to process the task reflects is mental difficulty
    b. that deep structures take longer to process
    c. that transitional probabilities account for syntactic processing
    d. that accessing the lexicon is the most time-consuming aspect of sentence understanding

(PAGE 33)

SHORT ANSWER QUESTIONS

1. Define *phonology*.

2. Define *syntax*.

3. Define *pragmatics*.

4. Define *neurolinguistics*

5. Distinguish between *language* and *speech*.

6. What are the three major questions of historical concern in psycholinguistics?

7. Define the linguist's term *universal*.

8. Give an example of a function word and an example of a content word.

ESSAY QUESTIONS

1. List and elaborate four ways in which human language is uniquely different from animal communication systems.

2. Describe the major components of a transformational generative grammar such as one originally proposed by Chomsky in 1965.

3. Discuss the difference between linguistic and metalinguistic awareness.

4. Discuss the concept of *universal grammar*.

5. Discuss some of the weaknesses which characterized early behaviorist accounts of language processing.

6. Describe and evaluate the *Derivational Theory of Complexity*.

CHAPTER TWO: THE NEUROLOGICAL BASES OF HUMAN COMMUNICATION

CHAPTER OUTLINE

INTRODUCTION
LANGUAGE AND THE BRAIN: A HISTORICAL PERSPECTIVE
    Early neurolinguistic observations
    Localization of function
FUNCTIONAL NEUROANATOMY AND NEUROPATHOLOGY
    Neuroanatomical structures involved in speech and language
    How speech is controlled by the brain
    Neural cells and their connections: the ultimate base of all behavior
    What can go wrong with the brain: Neuropathology
    Examining the consequences of cortical damage
LATERALIZATION OF FUNCTION
    Putting half the brain to sleep: the Wada test
    Splitting apart the hemispheres: commissurotomy
    Taking out half the brain: hemispherectomy
    Listening with both ears: the dichotic listening technique
    What functions reside in the non-dominant hemisphere?
    When sign language users become aphasic
INTRAHEMISPHERIC LOCALIZATION OF FUNCTION
    Measuring blood flow in the brain
    The role of subcortical structures in speech and language
WAYS OF VIEWING THE RELATIONSHIP BETWEEN BRAIN AND LANGUAGE
    Linguistic aphasiology
SUMMARY

KEY CONCEPTS TO EMPHASIZE

A. The field of neurolinguistics is primarily concerned with the role that anatomical and physiological structures play in the production and comprehension of speech and language. Neurolinguists are particularly interested in exploring where language functions reside within the brain and how the brain processes and produces language.

B. The relationship between language and brain function has been a subject of study since at least 3000 BC. Insights into this relationship have historically grown out of studies of people with head injuries and strokes. By the eighteenth century, almost all known language and speech disorders had already been described.

C. The first scientist to theorize that language abilities might be located in a particular part of the brain was Franz Josef Gall (1758-1828).

D. During the nineteenth century, Pierre Paul Broca (1824-1880) discovered that articulate language is typically located in the left third frontal convolution in the left hemisphere. This area is known as **Broca's area.** Patients with damage to Broca's area typically show symptoms of **Broca's aphasia. Broca's aphasics** have labored, ungrammatical speech and exhibit severe word retrieval problems.

E. Broca also discovered that lateralization of language is loosely connected to handedness, and commented upon the **plasticity** of the young brain in response to trauma, asserting that young children with damage to Broca's area may very well learn to talk.

F. Carl Wernicke, a neurologist who was Broca's contemporary, discovered another area of the brain important in language abilities. Damage to **Wernicke's area** brings about **Wernicke's aphasia. Wernicke's aphasics** speak fluently and their sentences appear to have discernible grammatical structure. What they say, however, often makes little sense, and is often filled with **neologisms**. Wernicke's aphasics also have severe comprehension problems.

G. The cerebral cortex is divided into two hemispheres that are connected by a number of fiber tracts, the largest being the **corpus callosum**. The brain itself is composed of alternating layers of white matter (nerve fibers) and grey matter (nerve cells).

H. Damage to various areas of the brain has been proven to have specific consequences for many different functions. Damage to the **dorsal thalamus** can produce **dysarthria** as well as aphasia. Damage to the **basal ganglia** can produce **Parkinson's disease** or **Huntington's chorea**. Damage to the **cerebellum** can produce dysarthria and **ataxia**.

I. Various elements of the **peripheral nervous system** are also important for language function, such as the **cranial nerves** which play an important role in **phonation.**

J. Speech involves around 100 muscles. Movement in primates is controlled by at least three distinct motor systems: one controls individual movements of the digits, the second independent movements of hands and arms, the third posture and bilateral trunk and limb movements. The motor control system of speech is probably the first system.

K. The brain is composed of **neurons** (nerve cells) and **glia** (glue cells). Electrical impulses are transmitted from one neuron to another across a gap (**synapse**) through chemical agents called **neurotransmitters**. Many things can go wrong in such a complex system: **neuropathology** examines the consequences of brain damage and disease.

L. Damage to various language areas of the brain can produce many different types of aphasia in which different skills are lost or retained. Patients with **transcortical aphasia** have no spontaneous speech but are able to repeat what is said to them. Patients with **subcortical aphasia** can speak, write and read normally but are unable to process spoken language.

M. The left and right hemispheres of the brain differ in their function. Although in the normal brain both hemispheres are involved in language function, bihemispheric involvement may not be necessary for reasonably good functioning.

N. The **Wada test** involves the injection of sodium amytol into the **internal carotid arteries,** which deactivates the **ipsilateral** hemisphere. Experiments using this test have shown that most right handed individuals are left lateralized for language. Many left handers and ambidextrals have bilateral representation of language, as do many people who suffered early left hemisphere damage. A very small number of people have right dominance for language.

O. **Commissurotomy** is an operation that destroys the **corpus callosum** and thus disconnects the two hemispheres. Studies of "split-brain" subjects have revealed that although only the dominant hemisphere can produce verbal output, many language abilities reside in the nondominant hemisphere.

P. **Hemispherectomy** is the removal of half the brain: a radical surgery sometimes performed on patients with severe neuropathologies. In cases of dominant hemispherectomy in adults, verbal output is very severely affected. If the surgery is performed on a very young child (under the age of about five), gradual recovery of language abilities appears to be almost complete.

Q. One of the problems with studying brain damaged individuals in order to determine the location of language abilities within the brain is that damage in one area may have consequences for functioning in another. **Neuroimaging** techniques have found metabolic abnormalities in otherwise healthy tissue located at a distance from the lesion site.

R. **Dichotic listening** is a technique developed to study the brains of healthy individuals. Different stimuli are presented to the left and right ears of the subject, who is then asked to report on what he heard. In tasks such as this, the left hemisphere processes words, numbers and nonsense syllables more quickly and accurately than the right hemisphere. The right hemisphere is more accurate when dealing with music and human non-speech stimuli.

S. Other functions that may reside in the right hemisphere include the ability to understand metaphorical and figurative language, as well as the ability to remember sequences of events or draw a moral from a story. Other paralinguistic functions, such as the ability to read facial expressions and understand stress and intonation also appear to inhabit the right hemisphere.

T. Some evidence, such as the fact that women tend to recover from aphasia more completely than men, suggests that women probably have their language abilities more diffusely organized within the brain than do men.

U. Techniques that attempt to locate functions precisely within the brain include measurements of **regional cerebral blood flow**, a technique first utilized by Broca in the late 1870s. **RFCB** measurement shows which areas of the brain are active when the subject is asked to perform such tasks as listening, speaking and humming a song.

V. A highly sophisticated method of measuring **rFCB** is a scanning technique called **positron emission topography** that provides a three-dimensional representation of blood flow within the brain.

W. A relatively new discipline called **cognitive neuropsychology** is a blend of **neuropsychology** and **cognitive psychology**. **Cognitive neuropsychologists** attempt to draw conclusions about normal cognitive functioning by studying brain injured individuals. The basic tenet of this approach is that the mind is composed of a dissociable set of **processing modules.**

MULTIPLE CHOICE QUESTIONS

1. The field of neurolinguistics is primarily concerned with
    a. the relationship between brain size and linguistic ability
    b. the role of neurons in language production
    c. the relationship between brain damage and language comprehension
 * d. the anatomical and physiological bases of speech and language

(PAGE 42)

2. The first scientist to show that language ability is located in a particular part of the brain was
    a. Franz Joseph Gall
 * b. Pierre Paul Broca
    c. Johan Schenk Von Grafenberg
    d. Carl Wernicke

(PAGE 44)

3. The nineteenth century neuroanatomist who first pointed out the difference between white and grey matter in the brain was
 * a. Franz Joseph Gall
    b. Pierre Paul Broca
    c. Peter Rommel
    d. Edwin Smith

(PAGE 44)

4. A brain damaged individual who speaks fluently, using sentences with a discernible
structure, but whose speech makes little sense and is filled with nonsense words is exhibiting signs of
    a. Broca's aphasia
 * b. Wernicke's aphasia
    c. Gall's aphasia
    d. Geschwind's aphasia

(PAGES 47-49)

5. The average human brain weighs about
    a. 10 pounds
    b. 1.5 pounds
    c. 5.5 pounds
 * d. 3.5 pounds

(PAGE 50)

6. For most individuals, language function is lateralized within the brain
    a. in the corpus callosum
    b. in the occipital lobe
 * c. in the left hemisphere
    d. in the right hemisphere

(PAGE 65)

7. Damage to the cerebellum can cause
    a. dysarthria
    b. ataxia
    c. aphasia
*   d. both a and b

(PAGES 52-53)

8. A patient with a brain lesion that disrupts communication between Heschl's gyrus and Wernicke's area would
    a. be able to read and write but not to speak
    b. be able to speak and write but not to read and understand spoken language
*   c. be able to read, write, speak and hear but not be able to understand spoken language
    d. be able to read and understand spoken language, but not be able to write or speak

(PAGE 60)

9. The surgical process of disconnecting the left from the right hemisphere is called
*   a. commissurotomy
    b. lobotomy
    c. hemispherectomy
    d. brain sectioning

(PAGE 65)

10. If the dominant half of the brain is removed, almost complete recovery of language ability is possible
    a. if the telencephalon is left intact
*   b. if the surgery is performed on a very young patient
    c. if there was no prior damage to the non dominant hemisphere
    d. if enough language abilities happen to be located in the non dominant hemisphere

(PAGES 68-69)

11. When an aphasic individual substitutes an inappropriate word for the one he intends to use, it is called a
*   a. semantic paraphasia
    b. malapropism
    c. dysarthria
    d. spontaneous production error

(PAGE 79)

12. Broca's area of the brain is
    a. the left side of the corpus callosum
    b. the posterior horn of the lateral ventricle
*   c. the left third frontal convolution in the left hemisphere
    d. the posterior third of the first temporal gyrus

(PAGE 47)

13. Transcortical aphasics are still be able to
*   a. repeat what is said to them
    b. understand what is said to them
    c. say their prayers
    d. swear

(PAGE 62)

14. One of the difficulties of using brain damaged individuals to pinpoint which area of the brain is responsible for a certain function is that
    a. the brain damaged individual may already have an atypical neurological structure
*   b. brain damage in one area may have consequences for brain functioning in another
    c. most individuals with brain damage have lesions in more than one area of the brain
    d. each individual brain may have its own, unique neurological structure

(PAGE 69)

15. Patients with right hemisphere damage often
    a. exhibit signs of aphasia
    b. have problems with phonology and syntax
*   c. have difficulty using and understanding metaphorical language
    d. all of the above

(PAGE 71-72)

16. As a consequence of left hemisphere damage, aphasia is
*   a. more common in men than in women
    b. more common in women than in men
    c. equally common in both sexes
    d. easier to overcome in men

(PAGE 73)

17. The process of deactivating one hemisphere by injections of sodium amytol (the Wada test)
    a. is used to pinpoint language deficient areas of the brain
    b. is used prior to hemispherectomy in order to determine which hemisphere should be removed
    c. is used on split brained patients to localize language and speech functions in the brain
*   d. is used prior to brain surgery in order to identify the dominant hemisphere and minimize the possibility of damaging crucial areas of the brain

(PAGE 64)

18. In a dichotic listening test, subjects are generally found to
    a. process all stimuli more accurately when it is presented to the left ear
    b. process all stimuli more accurately when it is presented to the right ear
    c. process words, numbers and letters more accurately with the left ear, and musical stimuli more accurately with the right ear
*   d. process words, numbers and letters more accurately with the right ear and musical stimuli more accurately with the left ear

(PAGE 70-71)

19. Sign language users with damage to language producing areas of the brain
*   a. exhibit disruptions of signing ability similar to the disruptions exhibited by oral language users
    b. preserve the ability to sign
    c. preserve spatial processing ability and thus most aspects of sign language ability
    d. preserve the ability to sign if and only if the right hemisphere is undamaged

(PAGE 73)

20. Linguistic aphasiologists use the term *module* to refer to
*   a. a processing element in the brain which is responsible for a particular ability
    b. a neural structure which is responsible for a particular ability
    c. a particular element of linguistic competence
    d. none of the above

(PAGE 80)

21. The Wada test clearly indicates that
    a. most individuals have bilateral representation of language
*   b. bilateral representation of language is most common in left handers and ambidextrals
    c. only right handers with early brain damage are right hemisphere dominant for language
    d. only left handers are right hemisphere dominant for language.

(PAGES 64-65)

22. Damage to which of the following subcortical structures has been shown to result in aphasia?
    a. the cerebellum
*   b. the thalamus
    c. the midbrain
    d. the cranial nerve nuclei

(PAGE 52, 79)

23. A patient who neither initiates nor appears to comprehend his native language and yet can repeat what is said to him and correct ungrammatical utterances
    a. is a global aphasic
    b. has pure word deafness
    c. is autistic
*   d. has mixed transcortical aphasia

(PAGE 62-63)

24. With which of the following conditions is aphasia **not** a common consequence
*   a. myasthenia gravis
    b. cerebrovascular disease
    c. Alzheimer's disease
    d. head injury

(PAGE 58)

SHORT ANSWER QUESTIONS

1. What is the difference between aphasia and dysarthria? Define both conditions

2. What is the most massive commissure connecting the two hemispheres of the brain? Describe briefly one of its functions

3. What is the motor strip and what does it do?

4. What are cranial nerves? What role do they play in language production?

5. What are the two types of cell in the human nervous system?

6. What is the Wada test and what does it do?

ESSAY QUESTIONS

1. Describe the difference between Broca's and Wernicke's aphasia. Give some examples of the typical speech output of both patients.

2. On the basis of what you have read, do you believe that animals could be taught to communicate in a human language? Why or why not?

3. Compare and contrast the results of left and right hemisphere damage on human communication.

4. Describe and evaluate the contributions of Pierre Paul Broca to the study of the neurological bases of communication.

5. Discuss how the study of cerebral blood flow can produce insight into how language is processed in the brain. In addition to the experiments described in the chapter, can you think of additional experiments you would like to perform using this technique?

6. Discuss the evidence that there is a *critical period* for language learning. How does the development of brain function and lateralization support the critical period hypothesis?

CHAPTER THREE: SPEECH PERCEPTION

CHAPTER OUTLINE

INTRODUCTION
THE HISTORICAL ROOTS OF SPEECH PERCEPTION RESEARCH
MAJOR QUESTIONS IN SPEECH PERCEPTION
    How do we identify and label phonetic segments?
    The *lack of invariance problem*
    How is speech perceived under less than ideal conditions?
THE SPEECH SIGNAL
    How speech is produced
    Place of articulation
    Manner of production
    Distinctive features
    Acoustical properties of speech sounds
        vowels: the simplest case
        acoustic properties of consonants
PERCEPTION OF PHONETIC SEGMENTS
    The role of speech synthesis in perceptual research
    Ways in which speech perception is tested
    Perception of vowels
    Steady state vs. formant transitions in vowel identification: an illustrative study
    Perception of consonants
    Phoneme identity is context dependent
    Voice-onset-time: an important acoustic cue
    Categorical perception of voicing contrast
    Other categorical perception studies
    Categorical perception: specific to speech perception?
    Other applications of the categorical perception test paradigm
SPEECH PERCEPTION BEYOND A SINGLE SEGMENT
    The perceptual outcome of coarticulation
    Perceptual effects of speaking rate
    Lexical and syntactic factors in word perception
MODELS OF SPEECH PERCEPTION
    The motor theory of speech perception
    Analysis-by-synthesis
    The fuzzy logical model
    Cohort theory
    TRACE theory
SUMMARY

KEY CONCEPTS TO EMPHASIZE

A. Understanding a spoken message is predicated upon the ability to hear and differentiate the different sounds that comprise the words of the message. Although the process of speech decoding occurs rapidly, it is actually a complex task that relies upon a number of distinct processes and is complicated by the fact that speech sounds have varying acoustic characteristics.

B. Speech perception research has its roots in the communications and military industries of the mid to late twentieth century. Much of the pioneering work on speech analysis comes out of the development of equipment for **speech synthesis**. The first device to decode and recreate speech sounds was the **vocoder**. The principles used to design the **vocoder** advanced the development of the **sound spectrograph**, an instrument that analyzes and plots audio signals on a graph giving a precise diagram of **visual speech** known as a **spectrogram.**

C. The **acoustical** properties of human speech are very complex. Understanding conversational speech requires the ability to process between 25 and 30 **phonetic segments** per second and to decode these segments into meaningful words. One of the greatest challenges for speech perception research is determining how we isolate and identify individual sounds in the complex speech signal.

D. Speech sounds vary considerably in their acoustic characteristics, both because of differences in individual speakers and because of the context in which they are spoken. In addition, speakers do not pronounce the same sound in the same way twice and the acoustic properties of fluent speech tend to be "messier" than those used to articulate a single word slowly.

E. The *lack of invariance* in the production of speech sounds makes conversational speech so complex and diverse that at present no machine has been created that is able to recognize and process speech the way that humans can. Some **speaker dependent** machines have been able to process relatively large vocabularies, while **speaker independent** machines can only process a very limited vocabulary, such as numbers.

F. Not only do speech sounds vary considerably, some speakers **underarticulate** words to such an extent that the words lose much of their identifying information. Other factors, such as lexical, syntactic and contextual information help listeners to understand such **ambiguous** speech signals.

G. Three major systems are involved in speech production:
    1. the **vocal tract,** which is the area from the **larynx** to the lips and includes the **pharynx**, the **nasal cavity** and the **oral cavity**
    2. the **larynx**, which contains the **vocal folds** and the **glottis**: the opening between the vocals folds where they vibrate to produce **phonation**
    3. the **subglottal system,** which includes lungs, muscles needed for inhalation and exhalation and the trachea.

H. The various places where the vocal tract is constricted to produce the consonants are called **places of articulation**. Common places of articulation for English consonants are **bilabial, labiodental, interdental, alveolar,** and **palatal.**

I. The source of acoustic energy for speech sounds comes from modulation of the **air stream** through the vocal tract. Some sounds are produced by opening and closing the glottis, known as **glottal pulsing. Voiced** or **phonated** sounds are made with vibrations in the vocal folds. **Aperiodic** sounds are created by producing turbulence in the airstream. Oral stop consonants are produced by stopping the airflow and then abruptly releasing it.

J. The rate at which glottal pulsing occurs during sound generation is called the **fundamental frequency.** The typical **F0** for men is about 125 pulses per second, for females it is about 200 pulses per second, and for children it is about 300 pulses per second.

K. Linguists describe speech sounds within the context of a system of **distinctive features.** All sounds can be characterized by their place of articulation, the presence or absence of voicing, etc.

L. The production of different vowels is determined by the **resonance characteristics** of the oral cavity or vocal tract during the production of the sound. The **spectrum** of the sound at the sound source (the glottis) includes the **F0** and even multiples of the F0, called **harmonics.**

M. Bands of **resonant frequency** change in relation to the movement of articulators during speech. These bands are called **vowel formants** and appear as broad horizontal stripes on a **sound spectrogram**. Consonants appear as vertical lines or columns on a sound spectrogram.

N. Men, women and children have different absolute values for the formants of given values, but listeners are able to process these sounds by using a system of pattern recognition. This ability is called **speaker normalization**.

O. The Pattern Playback machine used by Cooper, Liberman and Delattre in the 1950s was able to produce synthesized speech by playing back formant patterns drawn on a sound spectrogram. The researchers found that intelligible phonemes can be produced from highly simplified drawings. Manipulations of the data fed into the machine allowed the researchers to discover what acoustic cues are necessary for the identity of particular phonemes.

P. Research on vowel perception has shown that listeners most accurately identify isolated vowels when presented with the **steady state** of the vowel sound. In natural speech, however, vowel identification (which occurs between consonants) seems to rely most heavily on vowel duration and **formant transitions**.

Q. In both laboratory settings and in conversational speech, vowels are perceived more accurately than consonants, perhaps partly because vowel sounds are of longer duration. Consonants, particularly stop consonants, tend to be bound to vowels; the phonetic segment consisting of the consonant and vowel is said to be **encoded.**

R. The difference between voiced and unvoiced cognate consonants in the initial position appears to be highly dependent upon **voice-onset-time (VOT)**. The VOT for voiced consonants appears to range from just before the burst of air is made to about 30 milliseconds afterwards. The VOT for unvoiced consonants ranges from 40 to 100 milliseconds after the burst of air.

S. **Discrimination** tasks using voiced and unvoiced initial stop consonants present the listener with a continuum of sounds going from a voiced to an unvoiced consonant and ask the listener to determine when the voiced consonant becomes an unvoiced one. Listeners tend to hear many different **allophones** of the same consonant and then, at a certain point, recognize the consonant as different. This is known as **categorical perception.**

T. Studies of **coarticulation** of consonants and vowels have shown that when articulatory compatibility is possible, speakers engage in coarticulation, resulting in a **parallel transmission** of information.

U. Perception of words in fluent speech is influenced by higher level knowledge of semantics and syntax: **top-down processing** combines with **bottom-up processing** (using only acoustic information) to allow listeners to decode fluent speech.

V. **Listening for mispronunciation** tasks have shown that people tend to pay more attention to the initial part of the word than to its end. Sounds in a word are recognized sequentially: the listener accesses a word candidate and "fills in" the end of the word if it is missing or mispronounced.

W. The **motor theory** of speech perception posits that speech is a special type of auditory stimulus for humans and when we are exposed to it, we shift into a **speech mode** that enables us to link articulatory gestures involved in the production of a sound to the sound that we hear. Perceiving in the speech mode is held to be innate and species specific.

X. The **analysis-by-synthesis** model of perception proposes that we analyze speech by implicitly generating (synthesizing) speech from what we have heard and then comparing the "synthesized" speech to what we have heard. Little direct empirical evidence has been found to support this model.

Y. The **fuzzy logical** model assumes three operations in speech perception: *feature evaluation, integration* and *decision*. Listeners are said to have **prototypes** of words in their heads which must be matched to the auditory stimulus. This model emphasizes a continuous rather than an all-or-nothing approach to *feature decision:* the degree of the match is evaluated on *fuzzy truth values.*

Z. **Cohort theory** claims that in the first stage of word recognition the acoustic-phonetic information at the beginning of a word activates a *cohort* of possible words. In the second stage of analysis, all possible sources of information, including higher level processes, help to eliminate words that are not the target word.

AA. **TRACE** theory is based on a system of highly interconnected processing units called *nodes*. Each node has a resting level, a threshold level and an activation level. Phoneme nodes may excite word nodes and word nodes may excite phoneme nodes.

MULTIPLE CHOICE QUESTIONS

1. Which of the following phonemes differ **only** in place of articulation?
    a. [b] [p] [k]
    * b. [f] [θ] [s]
    c. [m] [n] [h]
    d. [w] [r] [l]
    (PAGE 97)

2. The phoneme [d] differs from [z] in:
    a. voicing
    b. place of articulation
    * c. manner of production
    d. glottal pulsing
    (PAGE 97-98)

3. A sound spectrograph:
    * a. displays frequency, time and amplitude information
    b. cannot analyze voice-onset-time
    c. is a vocoder
    d. produces synthetic speech
    (PAGE 91)

4. Which of the following does **not** contribute to the absence of invariance in the speech signal?
    a. coarticulation
    b. allophonic variation
    c. physical differences between male, female and child speakers
    * d. speech synthesis
    (PAGE 93-94)

5. Which of the following structures is **not** part of the vocal tract?
    * a. glottis
    b. palate
    c. nasal cavity
    d. tongue, teeth and lips
    (PAGE 95)

6. Distinctive features are used to:
    a. describe allophonic variation
    b. govern speech synthesis
    c. determine the resonant properties of the vocal tract
    * d. describe the specific attributes of the speech sounds of a language
    (PAGE 99)

7. Stop consonants are identified acoustically:
    a. by adjacent vowel formant transitions
    b. by voice-onset-time
    c. by characteristics of the burst
    * d. all of the above
    (PAGES 109-111)

8. If a sound is perceived categorically, then
    a. discrimination will be better than identification
    * b. perceptual discontinuity results from continuous changes in the physical characteristics of the speech signal

-19-

c. it is normalized by the listener
d. it cannot be synthesized adequately

(PAGE 113)

9. Results based on listening for mispronunciation tasks suggest that:
   * a. we pay more attention to the beginnings of words than to the ends of words
   b. we access possible lexical candidates only after we have heard all the sounds in a word
   c. context does not affect speech perception
   d. top-down models are inadequate to account for speech perception

(PAGE 120)

10. Which of these is **not** a common place of articulation for English consonants?
    a. palatal
    b. bilabial
    c. labiodental
    * d. uvular

(PAGE 97)

11. Motor theory of speech perception posits that the speech mode
    a. is innate and species specific
    b. is a special mode of perception that allows us to link articulatory gestures involved in the production of a sound to the sound that we hear
    c. allows us to hear sounds phonetically rather than acoustically
    * d. all of the above

(PAGE 123)

12. Early research on speech perception made the discovery that
    * a. natural speech contains many redundant sounds
    b. the ability to articulate a sound is necessary to perceiving it
    c. humans are uniquely equipped to perceive and understand phonemic information
    d. coarticulation of consonants and vowels is necessary for rapid and fluent speech

(PAGE 91)

13. Voice-onset-time is important in determining if
    a. consonants are velar or palatal
    * b. consonants are perceived as phonated or not
    c. harmonics are important in speech perception
    d. the speaker is male or female

(PAGE 110-111)

14. The rate of glottal pulsing determines the fundamental frequency (FO) of an utterance:
    a. men typically have FOs of around 300 pulses per second, while women and children have FOs of around 200
    b. men typically have FOs of around 50 pulses per second, women of around 100 and children around 125
    c. men typically have FOs of around 300 pulses per second, women of around 200 and children of around 125
    * d. men typically have FOs of around 125 pulses per second, women of around 200 and children of around 300

(PAGE 98)

15. If a sound is considered *highly encoded*, it means that:
    a. its perception is unstable
    b. it is **not** an example of parallel transmission of information
    c. it is coarticulated
 * d. its identification is dependent upon information contained in neighboring segments

(PAGE 109)

16. Although men, women and children tend to have different fundamental frequencies for specific speech sounds, listeners are able to understand all three different types of speaker because of
    a. voice synthesis
 * b. speaker normalization
    c. formant transitions
    d. categorical perception

(PAGE 102)

17. Studies of categorical perception have found that
    a. it is specific to speech perception
    b. all people, no matter what their native language, make approximately the same discriminations among consonants and vowels
 * c. bilinguals generally seem to have a single sound perception system
    d. changes from citation form are more evident in vowels than in consonants

(PAGE 117)

18. According to the fuzzy logical model of speech perception,
 * a. listeners understand words by matching them to prototypes of known words
    b. listeners understand speech through the activation of a complex network of perception nodes
    c. acoustic cues generate a cohort of possible words which must be narrowed down to the target word through logical deduction
    d. listeners can rapidly process messily articulated speech by using top down methods of perception

(PAGE 125)

19. Many phonemes which are perceived as the same are actually slightly different allophones. The production of these slightly different sounds is often the result of
 * a. coarticulation
    b. categorical production
    c. parallel processing
    d. misinterpretation of acoustic cues

(PAGE 93)

20. Using the Pattern Playback machine, researchers in the 1950s discovered that
 * a. intelligible speech can be synthesized using highly simplified spectrograms
    b. fluent speech has a highly regular spectrographic pattern
    c. vowel identification is possible even with a fairly simple speech perception machine
    d. natural sounding synthetic speech requires a fairly complex pattern of formant transitions

(PAGE 90-91)

SHORT ANSWER QUESTIONS

1. What do we call the portion of the speech production mechanism that provides the air support for speech? What does this system comprise?

2. How do we usually classify speech sounds in terms of articulation?

3. What is (are) the place(s) of articulation for the sounds [b] and [p]?

4. What is (are) the place(s) of articulation for [k] and [g]?

5. What is a *stop consonant*? Give an example.

6. What is a *fricative*? Give an example.

7. How would you recognize a vowel on a sound spectrogram?

8. Define the term *speaker normalization*.

9. What is a *bottom-up* model of speech perception?

10. What is a *top-down* model of speech perception?

ESSAY QUESTIONS

1. What is the *invariance problem* in speech perception? Describe the factors that contribute to the absence of invariance.

2. Describe the three major systems for speech production.

3. Describe and give examples for the following test paradigms in speech perception research: *discrimination* and *identification*.

4. What does it mean when we say that "phonetic segments are not like beads strung on a string?"

5. Distinguish between top-down and bottom-up models of speech perception.

6. Describe the *phonemic restoration phenomenon*. What does it suggest about the nature of speech perception?

7. Describe, contrast, and evaluate two theories of speech perception. For each, delineate what aspect of the theory seems problematic to you.

CHAPTER 4: WORDS AND MEANING:
FROM PRIMITIVES TO COMPLEX ORGANIZATION

CHAPTER OUTLINE

INTRODUCTION
WORDS AND MEANINGS: SEPARATE BUT LINKED DOMAINS
THE STUDY OF WORDS
    Methods of studying lexical organization and meaning
    Reaction time experiments
        lexical decision tasks
        semantic verification tasks
        priming tasks
        phoneme monitoring
    Naming/word access
        naming
        word association
        cued lexical access
    Speech error analyses
        tip of the tongue phenomena
        speech errors
    Word primitives
    Words as word primitives
    Morphemes as word primitives
    Evidence about word primitives
    Factors influencing word access and organization
    Frequency
    Imageability and concreteness/abstractness
    Semantics/meaning
    Lexical ambiguity and context effects
    Grammatical class
    Open/closed class
    Syllables
    Phonology
    Models of lexical access
    Serial search models
    Parallel access models
        logogen model
        connectionist models
        cohort model
MEANING
    Philosophical theories of meaning
    Reference theory
    Ideational theory
    Alternative theories: meaning is in the public domain
    Conceptual primitives
    Holistic versus feature views
    Variations of feature theories

              the classical view
              the prototype view
      Knowledge based approaches
            the exemplar view
            psychological essentialism
            psychological contextualism
      Contextual organization
      Models of semantic representation
            feature comparison model
            spreading activation network
SUMMARY

KEY CONCEPTS

A. Psycholinguistic inquiry into words comprises the study of the relationship between words and their meanings as well as how people organize, process, and access words.

B. Words and meanings are separate but associated entities. The fact that meanings exist independently of words can be proven in three ways:
    1. First, the *translation* argument, which says that there are some meanings that can be expressed by a single word in one language, but cannot be translated into another language.
    2. Second, the *imperfect mapping* illustration, which says that in any language there may be many meanings for a single word and many words that express a single meaning.
    3. Third, the *elasticity* demonstration, which shows that a word's meaning can change when it is found in different contexts.

C. The psycholinguistic study of words addresses three major questions:
    1. What is a word?
    2. In what form is information stored in the lexicon?
    3. According to what rules are words retrieved from the lexicon?

D. Lexical access can be studied using **reaction time** experiments, such as a *lexical decision task*, which measures how long it takes for a subject to distinguish real words from a list of nonsense words. This type of experiment finds that common words are recognized more quickly than rare words.

E. Some other reaction time experiments include *semantic verification tasks*, which require a subject to judge whether a statement about a category membership is true. In these tasks, prototypical members of a category are more quickly recognized than rare members of a category.

F. *Priming tasks* show how the lexicon may be organized according to semantic relations. Subjects recognize a word more quickly if they are "primed" for it by being presented with a related word first (i.e. "bread - butter"). Subjects may also be slower to recognize a word if they expect a related word to be the second part of a pair, but instead are presented with an unrelated word. (i.e. "bread - hammer").

G. *Phoneme monitoring* tasks ask subjects to respond every time they hear a particular phoneme. These experiments show that ambiguous words may prime listeners for several different words and thus complicate the lexical retrieval process.

H. *Naming* tasks ask subjects to read a string of words and non-words. Words are pronounced more quickly than non-words because their processing is speeded up by lexical access, and common words are read more quickly than uncommon words.

I. *Word association* tasks present a subject with a word and ask him to say the first word that comes into his mind. Adult subjects are most likely to respond with words that are semantically similar, of the same grammatical class as the target word, and, if the word is a member of a pair (such as "king"), with the opposite member of the pair ("queen").

J. Another major area of research on lexical organization comes from the study of speech errors. Studies of such things as *tip-of-the-tongue phenomena* give hints about the possible structure of our mental dictionary. Words of the same grammatical class seem to be stored together. Phonology also plays an important role: subjects tend to recognize the first and last parts of the word (the "bathtub effect").

K. Speech errors, in which subjects make "slips of the tongue" or substitute the wrong word for a target word also give some hints about lexical access and organization. Analysis of speech errors is particularly fruitful when studying brain damaged subjects who exhibit symptoms of anomia. Studies of the kinds of speech errors made suggest that words are organized both phonologically and semantically.

L. One view of the way words are stored in the lexicon says that they are stored as wholes and that each word forms its own **word primitive,** sometimes called a **lexeme.** A more common view says that words that are composed of smaller parts are represented by their constituent morphemes. This second view places an emphasis on *cognitive economy:* fewer units need to be stored in the lexicon because they can be rearranged to form a large variety of words.

M. The bulk of experimental findings seem to support the hypothesis that words are stored by their morphemes. However, while *semantically transparent* compound words such as "teaspoon" are stored as separate morphemes, *semantically opaque* compound words such as "butterfly" seem to serve as their own lexemes.

N. Some of the factors influencing word access and organization are the *frequency* that the word is used and the ability to form a mental image of the word (it is easier to access a word such as "apple" than a word such as "freedom"). Studies of patients with brain damage have also indicated that semantic categories of words (i.e. animate vs. inanimate objects) may be stored separately.

O. Words also appear to be stored based upon their grammatical class: in speech error analysis, nouns are substituted for nouns, verbs for verbs and adjectives for adjectives. **Open class** words are stored separately from **closed class** words. Words can also be accessed based upon syllabic and phonological properties.

P. A **serial search** model of lexical access, such as Forster's *autonomous search* model, says that words may be accessed through one of three major *access files*: orthographic, phonological and semantic/syntactic. Once the word is located through one of these routes, it must be checked against the input word in a *post-access check*. If the input word matches the word in the mental lexicon, the search is halted. If the input word does not match, the search begins again.

Q. **Parallel processing** models of lexical access, such as the **logogen** model, propose that words are activated to a certain threshold through all available input. According to this model, each word has a *logogen* of attributes that must be matched to the target word. Any logogen with enough of the same attributes as the target word is activated, and the logogen with closest match is chosen. The logogen model accounts for frequency effects by saying that high frequency words have a lower activation threshold than low frequency words.

R. **Connectionist** models consider the process of word retrieval to be analogous to the neural structure of the brain. These models are similar to logogen models in that they accept all incoming stimuli which is said to excite connections between *nodes*. When enough nodes are activated, the word is retrieved.

S. According to the **cohort model**, which deals only with the processing of auditory language, when we hear a word, all of its phonological neighbors are activated. The correct word is chosen by eliminating words that do not match the input stimulus, either because of more incoming phonological data or because of the context of the spoken sentence.

T. When we speak about the meaning of a word, we are talking about both the word's **intension** and the word's **extension.** The intension is the basic concept that the term implies: one intension of the word *chair* is an object to sit upon. The extension of the word *chair* is the category of object that could reasonably be termed *chair*, including armchairs, kitchen chairs, reclining chairs, etc.

U. The *reference theory of meaning* says that the meaning of a term is what it refers to in the real world. Two problems arise out of a strict adherence to this view of meaning: 1) it does not explain how two terms can have the same referent and yet have different meanings, and 2) it does not account for words that do not name things (such as function words), nor does it account for abstract terms such as "freedom" or nonreal objects such as angels. *Ideational theory* accounts for these things by saying that words denote ideas rather than things.

V. Just as there are several theories of what constitutes a word primitive, there are also several theories about what constitutes a *meaning primitive*. The **holistic view** says that concepts are stored as wholes, while the **feature view** says they are stored by their component parts, or features.

W. Three main views exist among proponents of the feature view:
1. the classical view, which claims that for any concept there exists a list of features that are necessary and sufficient to include an object in a particular category.
2. the prototype view, which says that the most typical members of a category

are used as reference points and that the boundaries from one category to another are often fuzzy.
3. the exemplar view, which says that specific members of a certain group stand as exemplars and that new members of a group are implicitly matched to known members.

X. Knowledge based approaches say that people have theories about concepts and apply these theories to items they encounter in the real world. *Psychological essentialism* says that people believe that things have underlying essences that make them what they are. *Psychological contextualism* says that items can be categorized by the context in which they are found.

Y. The *hierarchical network* model of semantic representation proposes that individual concepts are represented by *nodes* that are organized in our minds like pyramids.

Z. *Feature comparison* models postulate that concepts are represented as lists of *defining* features and *characteristic* features. All features are assumed to be stored under all relevant concepts. Semantic verification tasks are carried out by comparing the number of overlapping features of two or more concepts.

AA. The *spreading activation network* theory holds that concepts are represented as nodes, which are connected to related nodes. When a single concept is activated, surrounding concepts are also activated. Closely connected concepts are activated more quickly and more strongly than distantly related concepts.

MULTIPLE CHOICE QUESTIONS

1. Research that has examined the language performance of the Dani has been used to suggest that:
    a. language determines thought
    b. the Whorf hypothesis is correct
*   c. lack of lexical terminology does not affect perception of concepts
    d. the translation problem is not a valid argument
    (PAGE 135)

2. The "elasticity" argument suggests that:
    a. all words have fixed meaning
    b. function words are broader in meaning than content words
    c. not all words can be defined
*   d. the meanings of words are somewhat context dependent
    (PAGE 136)

3. Reaction time studies suggest that:
*   a. less frequent words of the language take longer to process
    b. it takes less mental energy to retrieve uncommon words of the language
    c. less frequent words of English are stored in a different location than more frequent words
    d. the meanings of words are elastic
    (PAGE 138)

4. A lexical decision task:
   a. requires subjects to recall lists of words
   b. asks subjects to judge whether a statement such as, "A robin is a bird" is true or false
   * c. asks subjects to judge whether a stimulus is a word or non-word
   d. is sometimes used instead of reaction time studies
   (PAGE 139)

5. Priming tasks:
   a. suggest that items are hierarchically arranged in the lexicon
   * b. suggest that items in the lexicon may be organized in terms of semantic relatedness
   c. suggest that a preceding word such as "nurse" will increase the reaction time for a following term such as "doctor."
   d. suggest that subjects easily confuse related items in memory
   (PAGE 140)

6. Cued lexical access studies suggest that:
   a. information about a word's initial letter lowers reaction time in naming tasks more than any other type of cue
   b. it is difficult to lower reaction times in naming experiments
   c. category membership is an ineffective prime in naming tasks
   * d. category names seem to prime members of the category, suggesting that semantic cues are more important than phonological cues.
   (PAGE 143)

7. Analysis of tip-of-the-tongue errors suggests that:
   * a. both meaning and phonology play a part in accessing and producing lexical items
   b. phonological similarity is the single best predictor of production mistakes
   c. once meaning is selected, phonology plays no role in retrieving lexical items
   d. phonological neighbors are rarely confused with one another in tip of the tongue errors
   (PAGE 144)

8. Which of the following will probably show the lowest reaction time in lexical access studies?
   a. a low frequency, high imagery word
   b. a high frequency, low imagery word
   c. an abstract low frequency word
   * d. a concrete high frequency word
   (PAGE 138, 149-150)

9. The logogen model of lexical access:
   a. is a serial search model
   b. proposes that high frequency words are stored separately from low frequency words in the lexicon
   * c. proposes that it takes less activation to access a high frequency word than a low frequency word
   d. suggests that low frequency words have low thresholds for activation
   (PAGE 158)

10. The category size effect:
    a. suggests that hierarchical networks are not very viable models of semantic representation

      b. predicts that the phrase *An ostrich has skin* will take less time to verify than the phrase *An ostrich has feathers*
      c. predicts that the larger the category, the shorter the search time required.
*   d. predicts that the phrase *An ostrich has skin* will take longer to verify than the phrase *An ostrich has feathers*.

(PAGE 181-182)

11. The *bathtub effect* says that
*   a. the first and last parts of words are remembered better than the middles.
      b. naming objects from a particular category primes subjects to hear the names of other members of the same category.
      c. phonological cues are usually more important than semantic cues for word retrieval
      d. slips of the tongue are often due to phonological confusion.

(PAGE 144)

12. Three arguments have been made to show that words and meanings are related but not identical. These arguments are known as
*   a. translation, imperfect mapping and elasticity
      b. translation, lack of specificity and elasticity
      c. translation, ambiguity and mutability
      d. translation, ambiguity and elasticity

(PAGE 135)

13. Semantic verification tasks
      a. ask subjects to supply the appropriate morphological endings to nonsense words
*   b. ask subjects to judge whether a statement such as *A robin is a bird* is true or false
      c. ask subjects to judge whether a stimulus is a word or non-word
      d. ask subjects to free associate from a list of common and uncommon words

(PAGE 139)

14. Which of these is **not** cited as supporting evidence for the claim that morphemes rather than words are stored as word primitives:
      a. the principle of cognitive economy
      b. multimorphemic words take longer to process than monomorphemic words
      c. people take longer to recognize "pseudo-suffixed" words such as *result* or *interest*
*   d. in speech error analysis, opaque compound words are frequently substituted with their component parts.

(PAGE 148)

15. Broca's aphasics are predominantly impaired
      a. in production of open class words
*   b. in production of closed class words
      c. in production of compound words
      d. in production of lexemes

(PAGE 152)

16. According to the exemplar view, how would one determine that a tomato is a fruit rather than a vegetable?
      a. by determining that it does not have all the necessary and sufficient features to be included in the category VEGETABLE
      b. by determining that is has all the necessary and sufficient features to be

      included in the category FRUIT
   c. by comparing it to a well known and prototypical vegetable
*   d. by comparing its features to those of several different fruits and vegetables
                    (PAGE 173-174)

17. According to the logogen model of word access, what accounts for the priming effect?
   a. logical connection between the nodes in the neural network
   b. the "spread" of electrical impulses from one logogen to another
*   c. a temporary lowering of the threshold of logogens related to the prime
   d. parallel access processing effects
                         (PAGE 158)

18. Psychological essentialism would cause primary school aged children to say
   a. that if you melt down a gold coin and make it into an ashtray, it is still a gold coin
*   b. that if you perform plastic surgery on dog to make it look like a cat, it is still a dog
   c. that if you treat a horse like a cow, it will give milk
   d. that if you see an older woman with grey hair making soup, she is probably a grandmother
                         (PAGE 177)

19. Which of these models of word retrieval says that the list of word candidates is narrowed serially as more phonological information about the word becomes available:
*   a. the cohort model
   b. the classical model
   c. the logogen model
   d. the connectionist model
                         (PAGE 161)

20. Ideational theory says that
   a. we have classically conditioned ideas about the meanings of words
   b. words refer to actual things in the outside world
*   c. words refer to ideas rather than objects
   d. the development of MEANING is an internal process, closely related to the acquisition of language
                         (PAGE 166)

SHORT ANSWER QUESTIONS

1. Define the term *lexical access*. What is the purpose of studying it?

2. On a word association task, a subject is more likely to respond to a word like *doctor* with a word like *nurse* rather than with a word like *sick*. A subject would also be more likely to respond to a word like *run* with a word like *jump*, rather than a word like *quickly*. Why?

3. What is *the-tip-of-the tongue* phenomenon and why is it important?

4. Define *anomia*.

5. The view that every word is stored as a whole suggests that each word has its own entry in the lexicon. What do we call these entries in the lexicon, and does current research support this theory?

6. Briefly describe a parallel access model of word processing.

7. Briefly describe a serial access model of word processing.

8. Briefly compare and contrast *defining* features and *characteristic* features as they relate to category inclusion.

9. According to the exemplar view, briefly explain how we might be able to deduce that a flamingo is a bird.

10. In a classical view of feature theory, how would we know that a triangle is a triangle, and are any triangles "better" than any others?

ESSAY QUESTIONS

1. Provide and evaluate the reasons why the terms *word* and *meaning* are not considered to be the same.

2. Consider the following sentences:
    "The men started to drill before they were ordered to do so."
    "The men started to march before they were ordered to do so"

    For which of these sentences will the reaction time to identification of the /b/ in *before* be **shortest**? Why? What is the name of this paradigm?

3. What is cognitive economy? Provide an example of a hypothesis about lexical storage or retrieval which purports to have greater cognitive economy than competing hypotheses.

4. Evaluate the evidence that suggests that morphemes are word primitives.

5. Summarize the various factors that seem to govern word access and slips of the tongue. What attributes appear to facilitate word retrieval? What factors appear to slow or impair word retrieval?

6. Summarize and contrast Forster's autonomous search model with Marslen-Wilson's cohort model.

7. Contrast the claims made by the reference and ideational theories of word meaning. What are the strengths and weaknesses of each?

8. What is a prototype? How does prototypicality affect the process of lexical access?

CHAPTER 5: SENTENCE PROCESSING

CHAPTER OUTLINE

INTRODUCTION
STRUCTURAL PROPERTIES OF SENTENCES
    Statistical approximations to English
    Where do people pause when they speak?
SENTENCE PROCESSING
    Syntactic resolution is needed for comprehension
    Surface versus deep structure
    Competence versus performance
    Syntactic structure and sentence parsing
    Clausal processing
MEANING IS THE GOAL OF SENTENCE PROCESSING
IS SYNTAX PROCESSED SEPARATELY FROM MEANING?
THE ROLE OF PROSODY IN SENTENCE PROCESSING
ON-LINE INTERACTIVE MODELS OF SENTENCE PROCESSING
    Shadowing and gating studies
    How on-line is gating?
WHERE DOES CONTEXT OPERATE?
CROSS-MODAL LEXICAL PRIMING
SYNTACTIC AMBIGUITY: HOW DO YOU PARSE AN AMBIGUOUS SENTENCE?
THE ROLE OF MEMORY IN SENTENCE PROCESSING
    Speech perception and lexical identification
    Syntactic parsing and retention of phrases
    Retention of semantic propositions
    What kind of memory?
A PROCESSING MODEL OF SENTENCE COMPREHENSION
SUMMARY

KEY CONCEPTS TO EMPHASIZE

A. The study of **sentence processing** examines how people are able to decode and understand rapidly produced speech at the sentence level.

B. The predictable structure of ordinary sentences, coupled with the relatively limited number of words that are in common use facilitate our ability to rapidly process speech. Sentence perception is, however, a highly active process, requiring a continual analysis of the incoming speech stream to detect the structure and meaning of the speaker's utterances.

C. Moray and Taylor (1960) demonstrated the predictive quality of English with an experiment in which they gave people several words of a sentence and asked them to fill in the next most likely word. The more words the subjects were allowed to see of the sentence, the more English-like the resulting sentence. *Sixth order approximations*, in which subjects were given five words and asked to guess the sixth, produce more grammatical results than *second order approximations*, in which the subjects were only allowed to see one word.

D. Noam Chomsky's theory of **transformational grammar** attempts to explain the structure of language, positing that every sentence is composed of a *surface structure* which is the actual expression of its *deep structure* or meaning. Sentences can have the same deep structure and different surface structures, or different deep structures and the same surface structure.

E. A complete theory of sentence processing must take into account both *competence and performance*. The average speaker of English has the knowledge to form complete and grammatical sentences (competence), but most actual spoken sentences consist of incomplete and ungrammatical fragments (performance).

F. In order to understand a sentence, a listener must *parse* it to determine its syntactic structure. The words of a sentence can be grouped into phrases that form separate *units*. *Trace* theory says that parts of a sentence may move from one position to another, leaving behind a "trace" in the surface structure of the sentence. In order to understand the sentence, the listener must detect this trace, thus reactivating the semantics of the correct lexical antecedent.

G. Analysis of the speed at which subjects understand sentences has shown that people tend to process sentences in *chunks*, or clauses.

H. Under ordinary circumstances, people will strive to understand a sentence as quickly as possible. While the surface structure of the sentence may be retained in short term memory, only the deep structure, or meaning, is retained in long term memory.

I. Early theories of sentence processing were based upon the premise that language is processed serially, with phonology, lexical processing, syntactic processing and semantic processing following each other in strict sequence, and syntactic processing being conducted independently from semantic analysis (*syntactic autonomy*).

J. **Prosody**, which consists of *intonation patterns, word stress, pauses,* and the lengthening of the final vowel in words prior to a clause boundary, plays an important part in language processing.

K. **Bottom-up processing** describes the way meaning is construed from the acoustic speech signal, which is separated into phonemes, words, and sentences, and finally processed semantically into meaningful utterances. **Top-down processing** describes how what we already know about what a sentence contains helps us to assemble meaning from bottom-up sources.

L. **On-line interactive models of sentence processing** differ from serial models by saying that all levels of language processing interact freely and continuously with one another. Some interactive models say that top-down sources influence the recognizability of likely words even before acoustic signals are heard. Other models say that top-down processes only begin to operate after sensory information activates a list of potential words.

M. Studies of the interaction of top-down and bottom up processes include both **shadowing** and **gating**. In shadowing studies, subjects are asked to repeat what they hear on a tape as it is being said. In gating studies, subjects are asked to guess a word both in context and out of context when parts of it are presented to them acoustically.

N. Gating studies reveal that people are able to guess a word within 175 to 200 milliseconds of onset when presented in context. Out of context words take around 333 milliseconds to recognize.

O. Modularity theorists believe that operations such as lexical activation are performed automatically and are *informationally encapsulated*. Early modularity theorists proposed three separate processing systems devoted to language:
1. the *lexical processor*, which activates particular words based on phonological or orthographic input.
2. the *syntactic processor*, which conducts an analysis of the sentence to create a surface structure representation
3. the *message processor*, which extracts meaning from the surface structure

P. **Cross-modal lexical priming** studies have shown that even in a highly constrained lexical-semantic context, all meanings of ambiguous words appear to be activated.

Q. *Local ambiguity* describes cases in which the syntactic function of a word is unclear, but eventually gets clarified as we hear the rest of the sentence. *Standing ambiguity* refers to cases in which sentences remain syntactically ambiguous. Otherwise ambiguous sentences may be clarified by prosody.

R. Although most sentence processing occurs quite rapidly, some sort of short term memory buffer which stores as-yet unprocessed words and phrases seems to be a necessary component of sentence comprehension. This memory does not appear to be the same memory system as that used for temporary storage of word lists and sentences.

MULTIPLE CHOICE QUESTIONS

1. The term *prosody* includes which of the following features of speech?
    a. intonation
    b. stress
    c. timing pattern
 * d. all of the above

(PAGE 214)

2. Which is an example of a reversible sentence?
    a. the boy read the book
    b. the clown threw the ball
 * c. the audience watched the clown
    d. the student took the test

(PAGE 202)

3. Studies of statistics of natural speech claim that the 50 most common words of English make up what percentage of the words we speak?
	a. 45%
* 	b. 60%
	c. 85%
	d. This is an interesting question, but no such statistics are available
(PAGE 202)

4. The two sentences *The child threw the ball* and *The ball was thrown by the child* have
	a. the same syntax
* 	b. different surface structures
	c. different deep structures
	d. the same deep and surface structures
(PAGE 206)

5. *They are eating apples* is an example used in the text to illustrate
	a. the distinction between competence and performance
* 	b. phrase structure ambiguities
	c. implicit knowledge of grammar
	d. "trace" theory in word movement
(PAGE 207)

6. The importance of clauses in sentence processing was supported by the fact that
	a. clicks could be accurately localized in sentences no matter how rapidly they were spoken
	b. clicks were not heard in sentences that contained many clauses
* 	c. clicks were heard as "migrating" towards major clause boundaries
	d. where listeners reported hearing a click in a sentence was not influenced by the sentence prosody
(PAGE 214)

7. The technique of presenting just the beginnings of words and asking listeners to say what they think the word might be is called
	a. shadowing
	b. echoing
* 	c. gating
	d. a lexical decision task
(PAGE 218)

8. Swinney's studies of cross-modal priming suggests that, when hearing an ambiguous word with two possible meanings
	a. only the meaning selected by the context is activated
	b. the meaning that best fits the context has the strongest initial activation
	c. the more common of the two possible meanings receives initial activation
* 	d. both meanings of the word initially are activated
(PAGE 224)

9. Martin's studies of brain damaged patients suggest that
	a. memory is not necessary for language comprehension
* 	b. there are probably different kinds of memory stores for the support of different kinds of mental tasks
	c. garden path sentences tax a person's memory span
	d. the patients could not tell who was the actor and who was the agent in reversible sentences
(PAGE 230)

10. According to the text, what percent of normal speaking time is taken up by pauses?
    a. between 5 and 10 percent
    b. between 10 and 20 percent
*   c. between 20 and 50 percent
    d. between 40 and 60 percent

(PAGE 205)

11. The experiment by Sachs in which people had to say whether a presented sentence was the same as one they had heard earlier, was used to support the position that
*   a. phonological and syntactic information fade from memory at a faster rate than does the representation of meaning
    b. meaning and syntax fade at the same rate as phonological information
    c. meaning is quickly forgotten, but the surface structure of the sentence is maintained in memory for a longer period
    d. syntactic information fades rapidly but phonological information does not

(PAGES 211-212)

12. People generally understand the grammatical rules of their native language, and yet most sentences they actually use in everyday speech are fragmentary and ungrammatical. This illustrates the difference between
    a. competence and production
*   b. competence and performance
    c. comprehension and production
    d. conversation and discourse

(PAGE 206)

13. Sentence processing is complicated by, among other factors:
*   a. unclear articulation of individual words
    b. the predictability of sentence structure
    c. the relatively large cohort of words in common use
    d. all of the above

(PAGE 200)

14. In a *third order approximation* to English, subjects would be
    a. presented with three words in a sentence and asked to supply the next word
*   b. presented with two words in a sentence and asked to supply the third word
    c. presented with three words in a sentence and asked to supply the next three words
    d. allowed to see the third word of several sentences and asked to guess at the meaning of a paragraph

(PAGE 203)

15. In everyday conversation, speech rates typically average
    a. between 60 and 100 words per minute
    b. between 80 and 120 words per minute
*   c. between 140 and 180 words per minute
    d. between 180 and 240 words per minute

(PAGE 200)

16. Interactive models of sentence processing differ from modular models in that
    a. modular models allow top-down processes to influence bottom-up processes
    b. modular models allow bottom-up processes to influence top-down processes
    * c. interactive models allow higher level processes to influence lower level processes and vice versa
    d. interactive models allow lower level processes to influence higher level processes
    (PAGES 216-217)

17. Which of these is an example of a top-down process:
    a. separating the speech stream into phonemes
    b. parsing the sentence
    * c. guessing at an unclear word from the context in which it is found
    d. generating a possible cohort of words from the acoustic signal
    (PAGE 216)

18. The latest research offered by Kintsch (1988) suggests that
    * a. propositions serve as important units in sentence processing
    b. clauses are still the most important units in sentence processing
    c. the ability to decode ambiguous statements can be represented on a coherence graph
    d. comprehension is an active process in which the perceptual system attempts continually to determine the structure and meaning of the sentence as it is being heard
    (PAGE 231)

19. The sentence *Flying planes can be dangerous* is confusing because it has
    a. more than one possible surface structure
    b. more than one possible propositional structure
    * c. more than one possible deep structure
    d. more than one possible clausal structure
    (PAGE 206)

20. The principle of syntactic autonomy says that
    * a. syntactic processing precedes and is conducted independently from semantic analysis
    b. syntactic and semantic processing are simultaneous and autonomous functions
    c. syntactic analysis may not begin before the end of a major clausal unit
    d. syntactic processing is separate and independent from phonological and lexical analysis
    (PAGE 213)

SHORT ANSWER QUESTIONS

1. Explain what is meant by *top-down* and *bottom-up* sources of information in sentence processing.

2. What is a *sound initial cohort*?

3. According to the text, what are two ways of reducing the size of the word initial cohort in on-line word recognition?

4. How would one define the *deep structure* versus the *surface structure* of a sentence?

5. What is meant by *competence* versus *performance* in language research?

6. Define *shadowing*. What does it show about language processing?

7. What do we mean when we say that a process is "on-line?" Briefly describe one experiment that would test this.

8. What kind of evidence is there that suggests that the memory needed for short term storage of words from lists is different from the memory needed for sentence comprehension?

9. What is the point of doing *statistical approximation* experiments?

10. Briefly describe the difference between *standing ambiguity* and *local ambiguity*. Provide an example of each.

ESSAY QUESTIONS

1. Psycholinguists have used statistical approximations to English to study the nature of associative strengths between words in sentences and between words in paragraph-length utterances. Explain how this works. Would such studies be more likely to reveal something about the Deep Structure of a sentence or the Surface Structure of a sentence? Explain why this is so.

2. What role might Working Memory play in the comprehension of sentences? What kind of evidence has been used to suggest that a normal short-term memory span is not necessary to comprehend the meaning of a sentence?

3. What is cross-modal lexical priming, and what has it told us about the use of context in on-line sentence processing?

4. How would the transformational theory of grammar relate the two sentences *The child threw the ball* and *The ball was thrown by the child*?

5. What is meant by the concept of Syntactic Autonomy in sentence processing, and how can it be contrasted with interactive models of sentence processing?

CHAPTER 6: CONVERSATIONAL DISCOURSE

CHAPTER OUTLINE

INTRODUCTION
CONTEXT
      Context of situation
      Activities
           contextualization
      Personnel
           participant status
           social relationships
           shared knowledge
PARTICIPATION STRUCTURE
DIMENSIONS OF CHOICE IN DISCOURSE
      Thematic structure
      Action
      Adjacency pairs
      Exchanges
      Preference system
      Closing
      Pre-sequences
      Social features
      Address terms
      Requests
      Social variation
      Key
TEXT
      Genre
      Stories
           reference
           backgrounding
SUMMARY

KEY CONCEPTS TO EMPHASIZE

A. Conversational discourse is language used in the context of a talk situation. Conversation between two or more people occurs as a joint activity, in which they alternate or collaborate in talking, thus establishing a **participation structure.**

B. Context, which is known before speech occurs, influences what is likely to be said, how it is likely to be said and how it is likely to be understood.

C. *Conventional situations*, such as classes, trials and church services, involve norms, specified structures, and special activities. The speech used in conventional situations is sometimes called a **genre.**

D. *Familiar situations*, such as the routines surrounding putting away groceries or talking on the phone, are a context in which participants have shared goals, but there is no established set of rules for participation.

E. Activities, such as cooking, knitting or eating dinner are also a context for conversation. Overlapping situations occur whenever there are two types of co-occurring activities with the same participants. In an overlapping situation, such as conversing and driving a car, sociable talk may be interspersed with asking for directions.

F. The participants' posture, vocal indicators, register, code, and choice of topic can indicate how the participants identify their situation and whether there is an overlapping, or potentially overlapping situation.

G. The dynamics of a talk situation are influenced by the number of participants and their role or status. The social relationship between the participants also influences what is said and understood. Another factor that influences talk is the amount of *shared knowledge* among the participants.

H. Conversational competence requires both paying attention to what partners say and making appropriate replies. Research on verbal turn-taking between American strangers on the telephone and in interviews, reveals that conversational turns only overlap briefly, overlap only at *transition-relevant places,* allow for very short gaps between turns, and specifically select the next speaker in the group.

I. Turn-taking studies have revealed that, for the most part, turn-taking is orderly, perhaps for utilitarian reasons, perhaps for politeness reasons. Researchers have suggested that there are two types of politeness involved in turn-taking: a positive form (listeners fill in pauses to agree and reply quickly), and a negative form (listeners are careful not to interrupt and thus risk long gaps in the discourse).

J. There are many levels at which choices are made by speakers. The choice of **topics** is made at every point in a conversation. Topics can be initiated, supported or changed. Topic control is said to reflect power. Continuity of topics in conversation shows a wide range.

K. Conversational engagement is expressed through **adjacency pairs,** which may consist of questions and answers, or initiations and responses.

L. Conversational exchanges occur both on a literal and on an implied level. According to Grice, people understand the inferred level of the conversation and supply the desired information based on the principle of cooperation. Another theory says that understanding is *locally negotiated*.

M. *Preferred* responses, which include accepting invitations, answering questions, and complying with requests, are supplied quickly and appear spontaneous. *Dispreferred* responses, which include declining an invitation or refusing an offer, are marked by silences, apologies, and preface markers like "well."

N. A common example of the structure of action is the closing of conversations. In a telephone call, each party takes several turns to closure, which can include finishing a topic, topic-less passing turns, optional appropriate endings, summaries or warrants for closing, and final farewells.

O. Preclosures, preinvitations, and prerequests are an indirect means of avoiding embarrassment to the speaker and may become conventionalized into **indirect requests.**

P. Social relationships among speakers are marked by linguistic features. This linguistic marking has been explained by two theories, one which explains these markers in terms of *power* and *solidarity,* and one which explains these features in terms of self presentation.

Q. Address terms in discourse serve two functions: 1) they call attention; and 2) they convey information about social relations or emotions. The choice of address terms depends on setting, age of addressee, kinship, relative status, gender, occupation, and marital status. Many languages have two or more pronouns of address by which respect or distance are clearly marked.

R. Requests are typically fitted into a sequence which includes attention-getters, framing moves, the request, supporting information, and a reply. Requests can be formulated as orders, offers or permission requests, and can be qualified with deference markers like conditionals and modals.

S. Mitigations in requests are frequently used when the speaker believes that compliance is doubtful or when the request is made outside the normal role of the addressee. Children of preschool age use mitigated requests, even with each other, and a study of flight crew communications reveals that lower status members of crews tend to make indirect suggestions to the pilot that are less likely to be understood.

T. The **key** of a conversation is its general tone of seriousness, task-orientation, levity and playfulness. Key constitutes a major cue for deciding how to interpret meaning.

U. Different types of talk, varying in vocabulary, sentence types, pitch and pronunciation are called **registers.** Special registers appear in many job and social situations.

V. In multilingual communities, different languages act like registers. Speakers engage in **code-switching** between languages, both when they change from one setting or situation to another (*situational code switching*), and automatically in informal conversations (*conversational code switching.*)

W. One of the first things we recognize about a conversational text is its **genre,** whether it is a dispute, a joke, a sermon or a narrative.

X. In narratives among friends, much cohesion exists despite a striking ellipsis of surface elements, and much is repeated.

MULTIPLE CHOICE QUESTIONS

1. Among the ways speakers indicate that their conversational move is **dispreferred** are
   * a. hesitation
      b. head shaking
      c. refusal
      d. fast replies

   (PAGE 253)

2. A street remark to a passing woman in New York can create a dilemma because of
      a. conflict between positive and negative politeness
      b. disruption of the conversational topic
      c. violation of turn-taking rules
   * d. conflict between responding to a summons and civil inattention.

   (PAGE 239)

3. Side sequences are marked by:
      a. deviation from the thematic focus
   * b. sequential transition markers like "anyway"
      c. intonational, stress, or rate changes
      d. all of the above

   (PAGE 248)

4. When two or more people are engaged in talk, they have a sense of participating in a joint activity, whether they are engaged in a personal conversation or courtroom exchange. This joint activity is called a
      a. familiar situation
      b. shared intent
   * c. participation structure
      d. context for exchange

   (PAGE 238)

5. A church service is an example of
   * a. a conventional situation
      b. a formal context
      c. an overlapping situation
      d. a text

   (PAGE 239)

6. Which of these is **not** an example of an overlapping situation?
      a. giving directions while driving a car
      b. talking on the phone while cooking dinner
   * c. giving a holiday party in a classroom
      d. turning a student-teacher relationship into a romantic one during a tutoring session

   (PAGE 241)

7. A recent study of American schools showed that members of different cliques in a high school mark their difference by:
   * a. vowel pronunciation
      b. turn taking rules
      c. adjacency pairs
      d. relative clauses

   (PAGE 242)

8. As compared to talk between friends, talk between strangers is more
    a. ideationally focused
    b. complex in its language
    c. formal
  * d. all of the above
                                                                (PAGE 243)

9. In an average telephone call between strangers, only one speaker at a time speaks
    a. approximately 99% of the time
  * b. approximately 95% of the time
    c. approximately 85% on the time
    d. approximately 80% of the time
                                                                (PAGE 243)

10. When important material is overlapped in a conversation, the speaker tends to
    a. increase his volume
    b. lengthen his syllables
    c. slow down or stop
  * d. all of the above
                                                                (PAGE 244)

11. Studies have shown that
    a. women tend to interrupt men more than men interrupt women
    b. men tend to interrupt other men more than they interrupt women
  * c. men tend to interrupt women more than women interrupt men
    d. men and women interrupt each other with equal frequency
                                                                (PAGE 245)

12. When one person greets another, the second is expected to respond to the greeting. This exchange is called
  * a. an adjacency pair
    b. a conventional exchange
    c. a social convention
    d. none of the above
                                                            (PAGE 249-250)

13. Which of these is **not** an example of a preferred response?
    a. accepting an invitation
    b. denying guilt
  * c. accepting blame
    d. disagreeing with another's self-deprecating remark
                                                                (PAGE 253)

14. According to the text, which of these forms is a conventionalized pre-sequence?
    a. a direct request
  * b. an indirect request
    c. an adjacency pair
    d. a telephone closure
                                                                (PAGE 254)

15. The general tone of a conversation is known as its
    a. subtext
    b. genre
    c. context
  * d. key
                                                                (PAGE 259)

16. When a bilingual speaker changes from one language to another in mid-sentence
    a. it is called situational code switching
*   b. it is called conversational code switching
    c. it indicates a conscious effort to identify oneself with the bilingual community
    d. it is evidence of incomplete mastery of the language

(PAGE 261)

17. The utterance "Would you mind terribly if I borrowed your car?" indicates that
    a. the speaker wants to know if borrowing the car will inconvenience the car's owner
*   b. the speaker is unsure of compliance with the request
    c. the speaker is of higher social status than the owner of the car
    d. the speaker is younger than the owner of the car

(PAGE 258)

18. In a conversation, when there is some obstacle to comprehension, speakers might repeat themselves or otherwise clarify the information to be conveyed. This is called a
*   a. repair
    b. redundancy
    c. restitution
    d. reparation

(PAGE 247-248)

19. When two people are in the process of describing something to a third, they tend to collaborate in the production of utterances. This is called
*   a. duetting
    b. overlapping
    c. cohesion
    d. ellipsis

(PAGE 264)

20. A series of linked arguments is sometimes called
    a. a cross examination
*   b. a dispute
    c. a polemic
    d. a debate

(PAGE 262)

SHORT ANSWER QUESTIONS

1. Give an example of the effect of situational or institutional context on turn-taking rules.

2. Give an example of how differences in the address system of two speakers can lead to misunderstandings.

3. Give an example of a contextualization cue for joking.

4. Why do responses and discourse markers like "okay" get borrowed into the second language of bilinguals, and even into the speech of monolinguals who don't know English?

5. What do the following two samples imply about differences in the context and the speakers?
>   (a) Good evening, sir.
>   Hello, Nelson.
>
>   (b) Hey! Whatcha doin'?
>   Hey, how are ya?

6. Some analyses of interaction use turns, moves, or speech acts as units. What evidence is there that conversational analysis must use larger units than these?

7. How are conversational features affected by solidarity or intimacy? Give an example to illustrate each indicator.

ESSAY QUESTIONS

1. Discuss the similarities and differences in the social meanings that can be indicated by choice of address term versus choice of directive forms. How do they relate to the Brown & Levinson theory of politeness?

2. In the following courtroom example, how can you tell that the selection is from direct examination by the prosecutor rather than cross-examination by the defense?

Counsel: Was there some event, Valerie, that occurred which kind of finally made you determined that you had to separate from your husband?
Witness: Yes.
Counsel: Did he try to do something to you?
Witness: Yes.
Counsel: What did he do?
Witness: Well, uh, he tried to kill me.
Counsel: All right. And then you felt that was the last straw, is that correct?

3. Define *formality* and give three examples of the conversational features (such as topic, turn-taking, action structure, address terms and other social marking features, register, etc.) that are affected by formal settings. For each of the conversational features you choose, describe differences between formal and informal settings.

4. How is high-involvement conversational style reflected in turn-taking procedures? Illustrate your response with examples.

5. Describe two types of pre-sequences. When do they replace a full sequence?

CHAPTER SEVEN: SPEECH PRODUCTION

CHAPTER OUTLINE

INTRODUCTION
    From concept to expression
SOURCES OF DATA FOR MODELS OF SPEECH PRODUCTION
    Speech errors
    Disfluencies
    Issues in speech production
WHAT ARE THE UNITS OF SPEECH PRODUCTION?
    Phonemic segments as planning units
    Phonetic features as speech planning units
    Syllable as a planning unit
    Stress in speech production
    Word, morpheme, and phrase units in speech production
    Word selection and placement errors
    Lexical search and pausal phenomena
    The morpheme and speech errors
    Grammatical rules
    The phrase as a planning unit
    How far ahead do we plan?
WHAT SPEECH ERROR DATA SUGGEST ABOUT THE PROCESS OF SPEECH PRODUCTION
    Speech is planned in advance
    The lexicon is organized both semantically and phonologically
    Morphologically complex words are assembled
    Affixes and functors behave differently than content words in slips of the tongue
    Speech errors reflect rule knowledge
SPEECH PRODUCTION PROCESSING MODELS
    The utterance generator model of speech production
    The Garrett model
    Levelt's model
SUMMARY

KEY CONCEPTS TO EMPHASIZE

A. The study of speech production attempts to explain how people turn a mental concept into a spoken utterance. Because of the difficulty of constructing experiments to reveal the complex steps in this process, psycholinguists rely primarily upon analysis of speech errors and speech disfluencies.

B. Speech communication may be viewed as a chain of events linking the speaker's brain with the listener's brain. Most psycholinguists would agree that the speaker's concept must be translated before it is expressed as words, but how exactly concepts are represented in the brain is still a matter of debate.

C. **Slips of the tongue**, such as spoonerisms, provide indirect evidence for the units, stages and cognitive computations involved in speech production. Study of speech produced in seminars, classes, and business meetings reveals that 2 percent of utterances are ungrammatical: this two percent provides insight into the production process.

D. **Disfluencies,** such as filler words, hesitations, repetitions, and false starts also provide insight into speech production. When describing pictures, hesitations occur roughly every five words. When conversing naturally, hesitations and fillers occur every seven to eight words.

E. Speech is produced by stringing together, arranging and rearranging a finite number of stored items. One of the major issues in the study of speech production is to determine just what those stored units are. Analysis of speech errors has show that utterances are composed of units of varying sizes and classes.

F. Speech error collections show many examples of phonological errors in which single phonemic-sized elements are **anticipated** (sounds which will come later on appear earlier than intended) or **persevere** (sounds produced early in the utterance reappear in an incorrect location later on.) Other errors include phonemes that are deleted, added or exchanged.

G. Phonetic segments as units of speech appear to be organized as vowels, consonants and consonant clusters.

H. The most elementary unit of speech production is the **quark**, which is composed of the *phonetic features* of the utterance. Phonological features errors are common. Vowel features may exchange or become confused with other vowel features and consonant features with other consonant features, but consonant features and vowel features do not interfere with each other.

I. Syllables also constitute units in the phonetic programming system. Initial syllables interact with other initial syllables, medials with medials and finals with finals.

J. Word and phrasal stress may also be processing units. Studies of speech errors in tonal languages show that tone can become disordered.

K. Word selection and placement errors are also an object of study. Disfluencies and hesitations occur more before content words than before function words, suggesting that the speaker has not yet arrived at his lexical target.

L. Morphological units serve as production building blocks. Stem morphemes, derivational morphemes and inflectional morphemes undergo rearrangement in different sorts of errors. The rules of inflectional and derivational morphology surface in speech errors.

M. Even larger linguistic structures, such as phrases, can serve as speech units. Sentence constituents (noun phrases, verb phrases, prepositional phrases) are marked off as units when we speak. Noun phrases and verb phrases may be exchanged in speech errors, but the grammatical structure of the sentence is not disordered.

N. Other support for the phrase being a separate speech unit is that in self corrections and retracings, speakers tend to go back to the beginning of the constituent containing the error.

O. Pauses are likely to occur at the clause boundaries, suggesting that speakers may need the pause time to encode the following clause. Syntactically more complex speech tends to contain more hesitations and filled pauses, suggesting that pauses reflect active sentence planning efforts.

P. Because from 79 to 85 percent of exchange errors occur in the same clause, researchers believe that speech is mostly planned in clausal units. However, the fifteen to twenty one percent of errors found outside of clausal boundaries show that speech planning must include larger segments of discourse.

Q. Theoretical, explanatory models of speech production must account for the hierarchical nature of speech production. A viable model of production must posit all and only the necessary stages of production and predict the form of the utterance representation at that level.

R. Substitution errors and blends suggest that words are organized both semantically and phonologically. Erroneous selection occurs only after the appropriate class of word has been selected since nouns substitute for nouns, verbs for verbs and etc.

S. Derivational errors in morphologically complex words appear to occur before *lexical insertion*. Morphological rules of word formation are therefore actively engaged during speech production.

T. The mental grammar accessed during production includes syntactic rules and constraints which determine which sentences in a language are well formed. Speech errors involving ill formed syntax must arise at the stage in speech production during which the syntactic structure of the utterance in being planned.

U. The *Utterance Generator* model proposed by Fromkin (1971) is a top-down generator that distinguishes six stages at which different representations of the utterance occur. The stages are:
   1. the generation of the meaning to be conveyed
   2. the mapping of the meaning onto a syntactic structure
   3. the generation of the intonation contours of the utterance
   4. the selection of words from the lexicon
   5. phonological specification
   6. the generation of the motor commands for speech

V. The *Garrett* model of speech production (1975) makes some of the implicit aspects of the Fromkin model explicit and provides a major framework for further work in the field. This model distinguishes between a conceptual level, a functional level and a positional level.

W. *Levelt's* model (1989) says that in the *preverbal stage* of production intention is conceived. The idea is then fed to the *formulator*, which includes both a grammatical encoder and a phonological encoder. The *articulator* then executes the phonetic plan by sending messages to the neuromuscular system. Finally, the *speech comprehension system* checks the output for errors.

MULTIPLE CHOICE QUESTIONS

1. Speech errors provide us with the opportunity to:
    a. evaluate the speedh of lexical access
 * b. identify the units used in planning and generating utterances
    c. observe the principles that govern speech comprehension
    d. observe the acquisition of phonetic ability
(PAGE 274)

2. Anticipation errors demonstrate that:
 * a. a sentence is not planned one word at a time
    b. Freudian psychology is applicable to the process of speech production
    d. syllables are unlikely to be basic planning units in speech production
    e. fatigue adversely affects speech fluency
(PAGE 277)

3. Studies of speech fluency indicate that:
    a. hesitations are most likely to precede function words
    b. pauses are longer before function words
    c. hesitation phenomena are less informative than slips of the tongue
 * d. hesitations are more likely to occur before less commonly used words in the language
(PAGE 281)

4. Which of the following is **not** a probable planning unit in speech production?
 * a. discourse
    b. phonetic features
    c. morphemes
    d. stress
(PAGE 276)

5. Patterns of retracing to correct speech errors tend to support which of the following as a possible planning unit in speech production?
    a. syllables
    b. words
 * c. phrases
    d. morphemes
(PAGE 282)

6. Freudian slips appear to suggest that
    a. the phoneme is the primary unit of speech production
    b. lexical insertion precedes assignment of grammatical class
    c. morphologically complex words are assembled
 * d. semantically related items are stored near one another in the mental lexicon
(PAGE 285)

7. An error such as *track cow/z/* for *cow track/s/* suggests that:
    a. the phonetic realization of the plural is assigned before the exchange takes place

-49-

    *   b. that there is a discrete stage at which the phonetic realization of abstract grammatical affixes is assigned
            c. the lexicon is organized semantically
            d. the speaker had unconscious competing plans

(PAGE 281)

8. Competing plans at the conceptual level might produce:
        a. hesitations before morphologically complex forms
        b. editing errors
        c. tip of the tongue phenomena
*   d. Freudian slips

(PAGE 285)

9. Which of the following is true of Fromkin's model of speech production?
        a. words are selected from the lexicon before syntactic structure is generated
        b. intonation contour is assigned after phonological specification has occurred
*   c. intonation contour is generated before words are selected from the lexicon
        d. phonological specification is the final stage in the speech production process

(PAGE 290)

10. Evidence for a monitoring function in speech production comes from:
        a. Freudian slips
        b. stranding errors
*   c. the fact that it is difficult to elicit speech errors which result in non-words
        d. filled pauses

(PAGE 295-296)

11. Errors in which a sound which will come later in the utterance inappropriately appears earlier than intended are called
        a. Freudian errors
*   b. anticipation errors
        c. phonemic preselection errors
        d. perseverance errors

(PAGE 277)

12. A lemma is
*   a. a bundle which contains the semantic and syntactic properties of items in the lexicon
        b. the part of a word that is mispronounced or otherwise misplaced in a speech error
        c. another word for a spoonerism
        d. a bundle which contains the phonological information about an item in the lexicon

(PAGE 295)

13. The Reverend William A. Spooner is famous for
        a. his revolutionary analyses of speech errors
*   b. his propensity for producing speech errors
        c. his model of the speech production process
        d. his data bank of speech errors

(PAGE 274)

14. If you mean to say *phonological rule*, but instead say *phonological fool*, this speech error would be called
        a. consonant anticipation

b. consonant repetition
* c. consonant perseveration
  d. consonant migration

(PAGE 277)

15. Which if these statements is true?
* a. syntactically more complex speech tends to be characterized by more pauses and hesitations
  b. telling speakers not to pause while telling stories has no effect upon their ultimate performance
  c. pauses and hesitations in speech are unnecessary except for purposes of breath support
  d. speakers who pause more while telling a story also exhibit more evidence of back tracking and repetition

(PAGE 283)

16. In studies of the speech produced in planned talks and spontaneous conversation, about what percent of the utterances produced are error free?
* a. 98%
  b. 88%
  c. 78%
  d. 68%

(PAGE 274)

17. When speakers are conversing naturally, how often do they hesitate and use filler words like *um, well,* and *you know*?
  a. every three or four words
* b. every seven or eight words
  c. every eleven or twelve words
  d. every nineteen or twenty words

(PAGE 275)

18. If, instead of saying *When you get old, your spine shrinks*, you were to say *When you get old your shrine spinks*, you would call this
  a. a Freudian slip
  b. consonant cluster division
  c. consonant cluster anticipation
* d. consonant cluster exchange

(PAGE 277)

19. If, instead of saying *big and fat*, you were to say *pig and vat*, this would be
* a. voicing reversal
  b. consonant reversal
  c. voicing perseveration
  d. voicing anticipation

(PAGE 278)

20. Analysis of the signing errors of ASL speakers has shown that
  a. they make many fewer errors than speakers of oral languages
* b. they make similar types of errors as speakers of oral languages
  c. they make unique types of errors, frequently "inventing" new signs
  d. they make many more errors than speakers of oral languages

(PAGE 278)

-51-

SHORT ANSWER QUESTIONS

1. What are the two major sources of data for models of the speech production process?

2. What are two common types of speech error? Give examples.

3. According to the text, what are the most elementary units of speech production, and how are they manifested in speech errors?

4. In a theoretical model of speech production, what do we call the stage at which words are placed into the intended utterance?

5. What is a *Freudian slip*? What would distinguish it from another type of speech error? Give an example.

6. Describe a type of error that might be produced by a speaker of ASL.

7. What evidence is there that word and phrasal stress are manipulable processing units?

8. Give an example of a stranding error

ESSAY QUESTIONS

1. Evaluate the suggestion that disfluencies are necessary for successful speech production.

2. How do psycholinguists determine which linguistic units are likely to be psychologically real components of the speech production process?

3. How far in advance is speech planned? Evaluate the evidence which suggests that speech is preplanned before production.

4. Contrast Fromkin's and Garrett's models of speech production.

5. What types of behaviors suggest that there is an editing function within the speech production process?

CHAPTER EIGHT: LANGUAGE DEVELOPMENT IN CHILDREN

CHAPTER OUTLINE

INTRODUCTION
METHODS: HOW DO WE KNOW WHAT WE KNOW?
- Pre-Chomskyan methods
- Diaries
- Wild children
- Assessment
- Contemporary methods
- Research design
- Interviews

THE COURSE OF LANGUAGE DEVELOPMENT: WHAT DO WE KNOW?
- Before speech: early communicative development
- Babies receive a special version of the language to learn from
- Infants learn about conversations long before they can talk
- Before they are able to speak, infants can communicate their intentions
- Infants have special abilities to perceive speech sounds
- Speech sounds show typical maturational pattern in infancy
- Early language
    - First words
    - Comprehension precedes production of longer utterances
    - The meanings of early words
    - Early sentences
    - Early grammar
    - Learning to make sentences in English
        - learning to say no
        - learning to ask questions
        - the role of word order strategies in sentence formation and comprehension
        - combining sentences
- Form and function as bases of language development
- Early social uses of language

THEORIES OF LANGUAGE ACQUISITION: WHAT ARE THE QUESTIONS?
- General features of theories
- Major dimensions of theories of language development
    - Nature or nurture?
    - Continuity or discontinuity?
    - Universal competence or individual variation?
    - Structure or function?
    - Autonomy or dependency?
    - Rules or associations?
- Theoretical approaches to the study of language acquisition
    - Linguistic/innatist theory
    - Learning theory
        - classical conditioning
        - operant conditioning
        - social learning

        Cognitive theory
        Social interactionist theory
        Connectionist models
PERSPECTIVES: WHAT DO THE DATA TELL US ABOUT THEORIES?
    Biological bases
    Biological, cognitive and social interaction
    Rules or associations?
SUMMARY

KEY CONCEPTS TO EMPHASIZE

A. Developmental psycholinguistics is the study of how and why children acquire language. Developmental psycholinguists have discovered that children learn language in quite an orderly and predictable way, and have attempted to discover the biological and social processes that make language development possible.

B. The systematic study of children's language is relatively new. Early modern studies focussed primarily on what children said, usually based on observations of the author's own children which were kept in diary form. Although diary studies can be a valuable adjunct to other research on children's language, they tend to focus on what is unusual or interesting rather than on what is daily and ordinary.

C. Other early studies of the acquisition of language were conducted on **feral children** or children raised in isolation. The most famous wild child was Victor, studied by Dr. Itard in eighteenth century France. A more recent isolated child, called Genie, was found locked in a closet in Los Angeles in the 1970s. Although both Genie and Victor learned some language, neither was able to master the language system, which might help support the theory that there is a **critical period** for language learning.

D. *Assessment* is based on data drawn from many subjects, and is used to determine clinically and educationally useful *norms* for the achievement of given milestones, as well as to describe gender and class differences and to seek answers posed by *developmental difficulties*.

E. Contemporary methods of child language research are based on the premise that the acquisition of language is a **generative process**. One of the most important studies, conducted by Roger Brown at Harvard University during the 1960s, studied the language of three children known as Adam, Eve, and Sarah.

F. During the 1980s, a large number of finely detailed transcripts of early child language were entered into a computer data base called the Child Language Data Exchange System (CHILDES). This data base enables researchers to examine and pool language transcripts already in existence.

G. Child language studies may be either *cross-sectional* or *longitudinal; observational* or *experimental*. Asking children direct questions about language (such as "What is your favorite word?") assesses their **metalinguistic** development.

H. Speech to babies is different in many ways from the ordinary speech adults use to communicate with each other. **Child directed speech (CDS),** in our society is characterized by *slow rate, exaggerated intonation, high fundamental frequency, repetitions, simple syntax* and *simple, concrete vocabulary*. Although the exact features of the *Baby Talk (BT)* register vary from language to language, BT appears in all languages.

I. Infants learn about conversations long before they can talk since caretakers tend to treat almost any sound uttered by the infant as a *conversational turn*. As the infant begins to acquire language, adults become more selective about what kinds of utterances they will accept as turns.

J. Caretakers tend to anticipate children's competencies and will *impute intentions* to their children before the intentions are actually there. Late in the first year, the child actually begins to demonstrate intentions and express them in *prelinguistic* ways that include *gestures, consistent word-like sounds, proto-declaratives* and *proto-imperatives*.

K. Infants are able to make fine discriminations among speech sounds as early as the first weeks of life, and are able to hear subtle differences between sounds that adults in the community cannot. By the end of the first year, when the child has begun to learn the sounds of the speech community around her, she loses the ability to discriminate among sounds not in her native language.

L. Language development in normal children follows a predictable course: until about 2 months, sounds are either *reflexive* or *vegetative,* after which babies begin to *coo* and *laugh*. At five to six months, they engage in *vocal play* (**babbling**). Around the first birthday, babbling contains many *reduplicative syllables*. Some children progress to a stage of **jargon babbling**, which may overlap with actual speech.

M. The first words spoken by children in communities around the world are similar in *phonetic form* as well as in *kinds of meanings that underlie them*. First words consist mostly of *open syllables* and tend to refer to things within the child's environment she can actively interact with. During the one-word, or **holophrastic** stage, children use a single word to function as a complete sentence.

N. At the earliest stage, children produce one meaningful word at a time, inevitably a concrete *content word*. At this stage, children understand more complex language than they can produce. They also typically engage in **overextension**, by, for instance, calling anything that can be sat in a "chair."

O. During their second year, when children have a productive vocabulary of about 50 words, they begin to put together two-word sentences. In English, these sentences lack articles, prepositions, inflections and grammatical modifications. Such speech is said to be **telegraphic.**

P. In English, where the root form of a verb can often stand alone, children learn the inflected forms more slowly than in languages like Spanish in which uninflected forms of the root are not permissible. The emergence of grammar is determined by a number of factors including the *pervasiveness* and *regularity* of a language's grammatical constructions.

Q. Brown and other researchers developed a measure known as the **Mean Length of Utterance (MLU)**, to track the development of language in children. The **MLU** is calculated by taking the first 100 utterances, counting the number of morphemes and dividing by 100.

R. Once children begin to acquire grammatical markers, most of them do so in basically the same order within a particular language. After children begin to learn regularized plurals and past tenses, they create some regularized forms of their own: this is called *overregularization*, and occurs in all languages that have been studied.

S. Acquisition of the negative in English progresses through three major stages: 1) negative markers, such as "no" and "not" simply precede the utterance; 2) negatives follow the main verb and "can't" and "don't" appear in sentences; 3) negative markers are placed on the verb auxiliary, creating forms such as "can't" and "don't".

T. In learning to ask questions, children usually learn well formed *Yes/No* questions before *Wh-* questions.

U. Young children learn the S-V-O order of English very quickly and have difficulty understanding passive and dative sentences that violate S-V-O order.

V. Children's first compound sentences use the conjunction *and*, and tend to link objects. Linking of subjects comes later, as does use of other conjunctions such as *but* and *because*. Embedded clauses are rarely used by children.

W. Cognitive, linguistic, affective and social development all play a role in language development. The early *social intentions* of language use include *drawing attention to the self*, *showing objects*, *offering* and *requesting*. Researchers have suggested that some children are more social in their use of language than others, drawing a distinction between children who are *referential* users of language and those who are *expressive* users of language.

X. Children's acquisition of *polite forms* occurs in conjunction with explicit teaching on the part of adults. Research on *pragmatic development* has shown that adults are less concerned with the *truth value* of what children say than with their using the appropriate forms.

Y. Theorists of language acquisition are divided on the extent to which language is *innate* and to what extent it is *learned behavior*. Other questions that interest and divide researchers is whether language is acquired in stages or as a seamless progression (*continuity v. discontinuity*), whether to concentrate on *structure* or *function* and whether a child learns *rules* or *associations*.

Z. Innatist theorists believe that the principles of language are inborn and not learned, because children universally acquire a successful grammar between 1 and 6 years of age, even without access to consistent grammatical models.

AA. Chomsky has posited a special abstract mental mechanism called a **Language Acquisition Device (LAD)**, that enables children to *attend* to the language that adults around them speak, *make hypotheses* about how it works, and *derive an appropriate grammar*.

AB. According to Chomsky's theory, the principles underlying all possible human languages are considered to be innate and all languages adhere to a set of rules known as the **Universal Grammar.** According to this view, children come innately endowed with linguistic switches, or *parameters* that they set once they hear the language of the community around them.

AC. *Behaviorists* or *learning theorists* claim language is acquired according to the *general laws of learning*. According to this view, language behavior is *reinforced* and *shaped* by adults. *Classical conditioning* causes children to associate words with things in the real world through the processes of stimulus and response. Through *operant conditioning*, language behavior is *selectively reinforced* and behavior that is not reinforced is *extinguished*. Finally, *social learning* causes children to observe and imitate others.

AD. *Cognitive theorists* believe that language acquisition is tied to cognitive development. According to this theory, children first learn a concept and then are able to "map" a word onto that concept.

AE. *Social interactionists* believe that biological factors are *necessary* but not *sufficient* to ensure language development. According to the social interactionist viewpoint, language is a *communicative behavior* that develops through *interaction* with other human beings. Interactionists stress the *functional* nature of language and study the interpersonal reasons children have for speaking. Interactionists also focus on the language of adults to children, paying particular attention not just to the special CDS register, but also to the way parents explicitly correct children's language errors.

AF. **Parallel distributed processing, PDP models** explore how information is built into a system through *neural connections*. According to these models, memory for experiences is distributed across many *processing units* that become connected to each other in a *neural network*. Children learn language by establishing neural associations between words and objects. Sufficient exposure to grammar leads to the establishment of neural networks. According to this view, children do not learn rules for language: the ability to do such things as come up with the plurals of nonsense words is the result of an automatic neurological process.

AG. Assessment of the data on child language acquisition supports the role of both nature and nurture: while it is true that the ability to learn language is innate, some properties of language are clearly taught.

AH. Linguistic capacity relies upon *neuroanatomical structures*. Left hemisphere specialization appears to be innate: cerebral asymmetry has been observed in fetuses.

AI. Language development is also connected to cognitive, affective and social development. The innate social and affective disposition of babies causes them to display many types of attachment behavior. Language use can be seen as serving the social and affective needs of both the child and the caretaker. Evidence that newborns recognize and prefer their mothers' voices brings up the possibility that babies begin to learn language prenatally.

MULTIPLE CHOICE QUESTIONS

1. When we say the children's early multi-word utterances are *telegraphic*, we mean they
    a. are immediately understood
  * b. include many content words and few functors
    c. include many functors and few content words
    d. are produced in a flat, mechanical tone of voice
                                                                    (PAGE 317)

2. Which of these words is **not** likely to be used by a child in the one word stage?
    a. juice
    b. up
    c. bus
  * d. truth
                                                                    (PAGE 315)

3. Adam, Eve and Sarah were
    a. chimpanzees taught to use ASL in a Columbia University study
    b. researchers on the neurology of speech in the 60s
  * c. subjects in a famous language acquisition study at Harvard
    d. "wild children" who never developed language
                                                                    (PAGE 305)

4. A research study that follows the same children over some period of time to observe how their language develops is
    a. a cross-sectional study
    b. a retrospective study
  * c. a longitudinal study
    d. an historical study
                                                                    (PAGE 306)

5. During the first year of life, the infant
    a. shows little ability to discriminate among speech sounds in the language of the community
  * b. begins to lose to ability to discriminate sounds that are not in the language of the community
    c. understands almost everything that is said in the language of the community
    d. imitates only those sounds she hears in the language of her community
                                                                    (PAGE 312))

6. Talk to prelinguistic infants
    a. is less rhythmical than adult speech to adults
    b. is found in only a few cultures
  * c. usually has higher pitch than speech to adults
    d. shows less extreme variation in pitch than does adult-adult speech
                                                                    (PAGE 311)

7. Infants recognize their mothers' voices
  * a. by three days after birth
    b. by six weeks after birth
    c. at birth if the mother is breast-feeding
    d. because of genetic preprogramming
                                                                    (PAGE 341)

-58-

8. In interactions between mothers and their three month old infants, the mothers
* a. seemed intent on giving the child a turn in the conversation
   b. expected clearly babbled sounds from the infants
   c. ignored most nonverbal signals from the infants
   d. grew more and more selective about what vocalizations they considered to be appropriate

(PAGE 311-312a)

9. The first recorded study of child language, performed by the Egyptian king Psammetichus and reported by Herodotus proved
   a. that children will learn language if nobody speaks to them
   b. that Phrygian is the most ancient language in the world
   c. that children cannot learn language in the absence of social interaction
* d. none of the above

(PAGE 328)

10. In our culture, adults tend to
   a. use primarily gestural, rather than verbal, communication techniques with prelinguistic infants
   b. carry on running monologues with infants, leaving few pauses for infant response
   c. address little speech directly to infants
* d. treat prelinguistic infants as conversational partners

(PAGE 311)

11. Most children begin combining words into multiword utterances when their productive vocabulary includes about
   a. 10 words
* b. 50 words
   c. 100 words
   d. 250 words

(PAGE 315)

12. A toddler who calls a cow "doggie" is demonstrating
* a. semantic overextension
   b. semantic underextension
   c. visual-perceptual difficulties
   d. inability to deal with arbitrary sign-referent relationships

(PAGE 315)

13. According to Brown's guidelines for calculating a child's MLU, compound words such as *birthday* initially should be
* a. counted as a single morpheme
   b. counted as two morphemes
   c. disregarded for purposes of determining MLU
   d. weighted according to a formula based on the child's age

(PAGE 320)

14. An example of a *parameter* in a language, according to Universal Grammar, is
* a. whether or not sentences require explicit subjects
   b. whether subjects and verbs agree
   c. whether sentences like "it is raining" can omit the verb
   d. whether or not sentences have a length limit

(PAGE 318)

15. When a young child makes a plural like *foots*, it is evidence that she
    a. has not yet learned English grammar
    b. is repeating what she has heard other children say
  * c. is acquiring the rule governed system of English morphology
    d. has developmental dysphasia
                                                                    (PAGE 319)

16. According to social interactionist theory, children acquire language
    a. by being exposed to language
  * b. in part through the mediation of adults
    c. because of an interaction of biological preprogramming and cognitive processes
    d. by being exposed to society
                                                                    (PAGE 337)

17. Studies of "wild children" have proven
    a. that there is a critical period for language learning
    b. that language learning is a skill that can be mastered at any time
    c. that children who are not exposed to language will invent one of their own
  * d. none of the above
                                                                    (PAGE 304)

18. A study of child language carried out in a laboratory in which a number of children and their parents are brought in and watched while they play with such objects as a doll and a stuffed bear would be called
    a. an experimental study
    b. a cross sectional study
  * c. a controlled observational study
    d. a longitudinal study
                                                                    (PAGE 308)

19. Which of these negative statements displays the **earliest** form of negation used by young children?
  * a. "No eat it!"
    b. "That not mine!"
    c. "Eat it no!"
    d. "I can't see!"
                                                                    (PAGE 320)

20. Nelson's study of individual style (1973) found that some children are more expressive than others. This means that they
    a. use language more than other children
  * b. use language that is more social in orientation
    c. talk about their feelings more
    d. spend more time labeling objects around them than other children
                                                                    (PAGE 324)

SHORT ANSWER QUESTIONS

1. When do developing individuals first begin to hear sounds?

2. List three common characteristics of "baby talk" to preverbal infants. Are these characteristics universal?

3. Describe briefly one language-related ability that infants lose as they begin to learn

-60-

their native tongue.

4. Do infants actually prefer to hear baby talk intonation? Describe an experimental design that can be used to test this.

5. What are two ways in which the prosodic features of speech to infants differs from the prosodic features of adult-adult speech?

6. Although an infant of seven months may produce something that sounds like *mama*, linguists would be hesitant to say that the infant uses this form as a word. Why?

7. How do children make their earliest negative statements in English?

8. What is the MLU? (write the words), and how is it calculated?

9. What is the LAD and what does it do, according to linguistic theory?

10. Describe at least one facet of language that appears to be explicitly taught to children. Provide a specific example.

11. According to the social interactionist view, what, if any, role do parents play in children's acquisition of language?

ESSAY QUESTIONS

1. You want to conduct research on a question such as 'at what stage and in what sequence do children acquire tag questions in English'. Discuss the advantages, and possible disadvantages, of the CHILDES database and computerized programs for the analysis of child language.

2. Historically, parents have conducted studies of their children's developing language by keeping detailed diaries. Discuss the advantages and possible shortcomings of this method.

3. Describe a study of child language that you might conduct using a cross sectional method, and one that could only be done on a longitudinal sample.

4. Compare and contrast the cognitive and social interactionist approaches with respect to the dimensions of nativism-empiricism, structuralism-functionalism and active-passive children. What predictions would they make if children were only exposed to language through television?

5. Discuss the evidence for and against the linguistic/innatist view of language acquisition.

6. According to a PDP model of language acquisition, how would a child know that the plural of a nonsense word such as *gutch* is *gutches*? Contrast this to how an innatist might say the child has learned this "rule" for pluralization

CHAPTER 9: A PSYCHOLINGUISTIC ACCOUNT OF READING

CHAPTER OUTLINE

INTRODUCTION
A HISTORY OF WRITING SYSTEMS
THE ALPHABET
THE UNDERLYING REQUIREMENTS OF READING
    Representational systems in word identification
        Learning systems
            semantic coding
            phonological coding
            syntactic/grammatical coding
        The visual system
        Motor systems
    Cognitive processes involved in reading and all learning
        Attention
        Associative learning
        Cross-modal transfer
        Pattern analysis and rule learning
        Serial memory
THE DEVELOPMENT OF READING
    The protoliteracy period
    Phonological skills
    Vocabulary knowledge
    Letter recognition and naming speed abilities
    Stages of literacy
MODELS OF SKILLED READING
    Context driven "top down" models
    Stimulus driven "bottom up" models
    Whole word models
    Component letter models
    Syllabic units
    Multilevel and parallel coding systems models
    La Berge and Samuels' multilevel coding model
    Parallel coding system models
    Activation or logogen models
    Morton's logogen model
    Interactive activation and connectionist models
    Lexical search models
SUMMARY

KEY CONCEPTS TO EMPHASIZE

A. The acquisition of written language has changed our species in fundamental ways. The development of reading and writing is intimately connected to the development of oral language, and the study of written language cannot be dissociated from the study of oral language.

B. The earliest known writing system was devised around 4000 BC by the ancient Sumerians, who used **pictographs** to represent ideas or concepts. Chinese **ideograms** (symbols that signify ideas or things but not particular words for them) appeared around 2000 BC and were used for religious purposes. Early Mayans also used a picture writing system.

C. The move from pictures that represent ideas to symbols that represent words marks the beginning of true writing systems. Various scholars have proposed a relatively orderly progression from **logographs** (e.g. Egyptian hieroglyphics) to **syllabaries** (e. g. Japanese Kana) to **alphabets** (e.g. systems in which each **grapheme** represents a **phoneme**.)

D. All modern alphabets are based upon the Greek alphabet. This alphabet was adapted from the syllable-based Phoenician system and made into a phoneme-based system. Three conditions for a true alphabet are:
 1. each phoneme in the language must be represented in the writing system
 2. there should be an unambiguous phoneme-grapheme correspondence
 3. the total number of graphemes in the system should be limited

E. The extensive use of written language in the ancient world began to make explicit some of the tacit aspects of knowledge carried by oral language and brought with it two critical consequences:
 1. an ordering and a rethinking of previous knowledge
 2. a new distinction between factual information and its interpretation.
Olsen (1986) claims that the split between what is given in the text and how it is interpreted by the reader is the basis for modern science and an awareness of subjectivity.

F. A child learning to read invests printed words with different types of linguistic properties derived from corresponding linguistic *codes*, such as *semantic codes, phonological codes* and *syntactic/grammatical codes*.

G. *Semantic codes* are the interconnected mental representations of meanings assigned to words and units of language. In order for a child to associate a meaning with a printed word, he must adequately understand that word, especially at the beginning stages of reading.

H. *Phonological codes* are abstract mental representations of the sound attributes of spoken and written words along with implicit rules for ordering and combining them (phonotactics). Phonological coding aids in **segmentation** of spoken and printed words, and promotes the development of **morphophonemic production rules.**

I. *Syntactic codes* are abstract representations containing rules for making sentences. *Grammatical codes* are representations of the word's grammatical class. Competence in grammar and syntax facilitates word identification by:
 1. aiding the child in anticipating which words might appear in given sentence frames
 2. aiding the child in assigning *function codes* to define a word's unique role in a sentence
 3. aiding the child in understanding and correctly pronouncing words containing derivational morphemes

J. Developing readers must use the visual system to discriminate among thousands of printed words. The successful reader acquires a number of synthesizing strategies that reduce the load on visual memory. Taking advantage of frequently occurring spelling-sound correspondences, they:
   1. store rules for the order in which letters may occur
   2. store rules for ordering letters in words
   3. store representations of redundant spellings and pronunciations (the *at* in *cat* and *fat*)
   4. make fine grained discriminations among visually similar words
   5. store representations of morphophonemic units with invariant spellings and pronunciations
   6. store unitized representations of redundant combinations of letters
   7. identify new words through recombination of known words

K. In word identification, the language system is predominant over the visual system. The language system facilitates synthesis of the visual information needed to acquire fluency in word identification.

L. Success in learning to read is highly dependent upon attention. Children must learn to become efficient in attending selectively (**perceptual learning**) by having:
   1. a conscious motivation to learn
   2. an emotional or affective state that permits them to attend
   3. enough knowledge to facilitate selective attention and make critical discriminations

M. **Association** (the ability to establish connective bond between written and spoken language) involves a search for **implicit mediators** (retrieval cues) that may link two associates in a semantic network. Associative learning usually appears to be a gradual and natural process.

N. Reading involves connecting representations stored in one system (such as the mental representation of a spoken word) with representations stored in another (such as the mental representation of a written word). This is known as **cross-modal transfer** or **intersensory integration.**

O. Another ability highly important in reading is the ability to detect *pattern invariance*. Gibson (1969) suggests that we are automatically programmed to search for invariant patterns and thus utilize spelling-sound correspondences and redundancies even if we are not explicitly looking for them.

P. **Serial memory** is a generalized ability that determines the order in which all information is processed. Some investigators have posited that serial memory is a neurologically distinct capability located in the left hemisphere.

Q. Two strategies most often used to serialize random arrays are *chunking* (reducing the size of the array by grouping information into units) and *recoding* (assigning the grouped units superordinate codes that facilitate recovery of position and item information.) Serial recall is almost always rule based. In learning to read, children serialize the letters in a printed word by using spelling-sound correspondences and recognizing orthographic redundancy.

R. The attainment of reading skills in children is rooted in spoken language skills. A preliterate child's phonological skills and ability to recognize letters are the best predictors of her reading achievement.

S. Children whose parents read to them during the protoliterate period develop the skills necessary for reading. Children learn to make a correspondences between print and sound, to recognize rhyme and alliteration, and to understand that words are made up of phonological parts. Finally, children who are read to develop higher vocabularies.

T. Early reading experiences include making attempts to read familiar books and to write stories. In early writing, children use their own invented spellings, which may reflect what they do or do not hear in the speech stream.

U. The development of phonological skills during the protoliteracy period begins with the ability to segment syllables, and progresses to learning *onset* and *rime*, and finally to the ability to segment phonemes.

V. The ability to read and segmentation proficiency have a *bidirectional* influence upon each other. Bidirectional relationships with reading are also found in vocabulary and letter recognition skills.

W. The speed of naming letters or numbers is a powerful predictor of later reading in kindergarten children. After reading is acquired, the speed of letter naming quickly reaches almost adult levels. A deficit in naming speed is a *specific deficit* found in dyslexic readers.

X. According to Ehri (1985) and Chall (1983), the earliest stage of reading development is centered upon letter discrimination and recognition. According to Ehri, young children build up a repertoire of letter sound correspondences that provide the basis for the move from pre-reader to reader.

Y. In the **logographic** stage that follows, highly familiar words are recognized visually. During this period, there is a general dissociation between reading and writing, since children's invented spellings continue to be phonologically based, whereas their reading strategies are visually based. Children in this stage frequently cannot read what they write.

Z. During what Frith (1985) refers to as the *alphabetic phase*, children begin a more systematic learning of grapheme-phoneme rules. During this phase, lower level skills are practiced and made automatic.

AA. During the final **orthographic** phase of literacy acquisition, the reader acquires morphophonemic knowledge, learns to use analogies and to understand how context dictates pronunciation rules.

AB. Context driven models of word recognition in adult readers assume that higher level information can directly affect the way lower-level stimulus is perceived. According to these models, words are recognized by their orthographic features only after the context has allowed the reader to predict what words or types of word he might encounter.

AC. Stimulus driven (bottom-up) models assume that word recognition depends upon information in the actual printed word. Bottom up models recognize three separate stages: 1) a *sensory stage* where the visual features are extracted, 2) a *recognition stage* where a representation of the word is accessed, and 3) an *interpretive stage* where the meaning is accessed.

AD. *Whole word* models postulate that printed words are represented mentally as wholes and a word is recognized by a pattern of features.

AE. Component letter models postulate that all of a word's letters must be recognized and the letters are then phonologically encoded into words through either serial or parallel processing. Another model that relies upon phonological recoding posits that the basic units of recognition are phonologically defined syllables called *Vocalic Center Groups (VCG units)*.

AF. Multilevel coding models postulate that word recognition involves learning hierarchically ordered "codes" for features, spelling patterns, etc. These codes become *unitized* through perceptual learning and recognizing them becomes automatic so that attention can be focussed upon assembling the codes at the next level.

AG. Other reading models are fashioned after those used to explain word recognition, and include a logogen model, and an *interactive-activation* model, a **parallel distributed processing (PDP)** model, and a lexical search model.

MULTIPLE CHOICE QUESTIONS

1. Which of these is an example of a logographic system?
   - a. ancient Phoenician writing
   - * b. ancient Egyptian hieroglyphs
   - c. modern Japanese Kana
   - d. ancient Mayan picture writing

   (PAGE 353)

2. What, according to Havelock, is necessary for a true alphabetic system?
   - a. a one to one phoneme-grapheme correspondence
   - b. a relatively small total number of graphemes
   - c. that every phoneme in the language is covered by the system
   - * d. all of the above

   (PAGES 353-354)

3. Children's invented spellings indicate that
   - a. they have not had proper writing instruction
   - b. they are as yet unable to make phoneme-grapheme correspondences
   - * c. they are in the process of trying to decode the written system through linguistic guesswork
   - d. they are probably dyslexic

   (PAGE 365)

4. Research conducted on children learning to read has shown that
*   a. the visual system takes its lead from the language system in learning to decode written symbols
   b. children learning to read will learn faster if they are only exposed to one typographic font
   c. children will learn to read faster if they are only exposed to words written either in all capitals or all small letters
   d. children cannot learn to read until they have complete mastery over the alphabet

(PAGE 359)

5. Interactive reading models suggest that
*   a. meaning is understood when a sufficient threshold of information is reached
   b. components in the reading process operate serially, from the bottom up
   c. components in the reading process operate serially, from the top down
   d. interaction with literate adults, rather than formal instruction, is the most efficient way to learn to read

(PAGE 379)

6. Which of these has been shown to be a powerful indicator of future reading success among kindergarten children?
*   a. the speed of letter and number naming
   b. clear, precise orthography
   c. the ability to repeat what is said to them
   d. all of the above

(PAGE 367)

7. According to Morton's logogen model of reading
   a. words are recognized through a dual route that includes both GPC rules and direct access to lexical representations
*   b. words are recognized when their characteristics reach a certain threshold of activation
   c. words are accessed by being searched for serially in an orthographic access file
   d. none of the above

(PAGE 378)

8. When a child is in the logographic stage described by Frith (1985), she might be able to
*   a. write, but not be able to read what she writes
   b. read familiar books
   c. "sound out" unfamiliar words
   d. correct her phonological spelling

(PAGE 368)

9. According to Gibson (1969), how do children learn to detect patterns in word spelling
   a. through rote study
   b. through cross-modal transfer
   c. through parental intervention
*   d. through the naturally programmed tendency to search for pattern invariance

(PAGE 362)

10. Children are more likely to learn to read quickly
    * a. if their parents read to them
    b. if their parents encourage them to use proper spelling
    c. if their parents leave books around
    d. if they are not exposed to picture books
    (PAGE 365)

11. Top-down processes include
    a. recognizing letters
    * b. recognizing orthographic redundancies
    c. processing grapheme-phoneme correspondences
    d. all of the above
    (PAGE 373)

12. Upon what alphabet are all modern alphabets based?
    a. the Phoenician alphabet
    b. the Arabic alphabet
    * c. the Greek alphabet
    d. the Latin alphabet
    (PAGE 353)

13. When we say that reading is an *automatic* process, we mean that
    * a. it requires no conscious effort
    b. it is easily learned
    c. it can be self taught
    d. it requires a transparent relationship between symbols and sounds
    (PAGE 354)

14. Studies have shown that vocabulary knowledge in developing readers
    a. has no effect upon lower level reading processes
    * b. augments and is augmented by reading experience
    c. is indicative of the reader's metalinguistic ability
    d. is highly correlated with letter recognition skills
    (PAGE 366)

15. Dyslexic adults have been shown
    a. to have defects in the visual system
    b. to have various cognitive and social deficits
    * c. to have a specific deficit in letter naming speed
    d. all of the above
    (PAGE 367)

16. What word would be **most likely** to be among the first words a child would learn to recognize?
    * a. her own name
    b. simple, concrete words such as "bus" and "juice"
    c. words for things she likes, such as "cookie"
    d. words she is specifically taught
    (PAGE 367)

17. In the third grade, the normally developing child reader would be expected to
    a. learn to make more systematic grapheme-phoneme correspondences
    * b. begin directing his attention to meaning and inference
    c. concentrate on recognizing perspective in what he reads
    d. begin to actively synthesize different bodies of knowledge
    (PAGE 370)

18. The ability to attend selectively to the distinguishing attributes of letters and words is part of
      a. semantic coding
      b. cognitive processing
*   c. perceptual learning
      d. fine visual discrimination

(PAGE 360)

19. What has been cited as evidence for the dual route model of word access?
*   a. the fact that skilled readers are able to name printed words faster than printed non-words
      b. the fact that skilled readers tend to remember the phonological properties of passages they have read as well as the semantic properties
      c. the fact that workers in artificial intelligence have been able to devise impressive computer simulations of word recognition phenomena
      d. the fact that, in brain damaged patients with reading disturbances, phonological confusion and semantic confusion are always co-present

(PAGE 377)

20. Establishing a connective bond between the visual symbol for a word and the mental concept of that word's meaning is called
*   a. cross-modal transfer
      b. perceptual learning
      c. semantic association
      d. automatic co-processing

(PAGE 362)

SHORT ANSWER QUESTIONS

1. Describe briefly the main difference between writing systems that use syllabaries and those that use alphabets.

2. What are two major components of the alphabetic principle that give alphabetic writing systems their advantage over other ways of representing language through writing?

3. English spelling is less "transparent" than the systems used by Spanish or Serbo-Croatian. What possible advantage do researchers see in maintaining spellings like "sign"?

4. Describe two ways in which reading to a young child is thought to contribute to the attainment of literacy.

5. Do teaching methods that emphasize phonics emphasize "top down" or "bottom up" processes? Explain.

6. Studies have shown that skilled readers are faster at naming frequent words than pseudo-words (e.g., "money" is read aloud faster than "yomen"). What kind of theory of representation has been used to explain this?

7. How, according to a serial processing model, are words read?

8. What are the differences between lower-level and higher-level processes in reading?

ESSAY QUESTIONS

1. Discuss the kinds of experiences that adults can provide for children that enhance children's attainment of reading. What are some early predictors in children of later reading success?

2. A skilled reader is asked to read aloud a sentence containing both very familiar and very rare words. How does a dual route model such as Coultheart's account for successful production of the sentence?

3. Discuss the advantages that parallel processing models have over serial models when describing the reading process.

4. Discuss the kinds of intellectual advantages that the establishment of writing brought to the human race, with particular reference to the kinds of thought available to literate societies that may not be found in purely oral cultures.

5. Describe with reference to the models you have studied the differences in processing that occur when a young reader and an older skilled reader read words.

6. Models of reading processes have become increasingly complex and various. What are some of the basic components in most models and why are theoretical models important for real children?

CHAPTER 10: BILINGUALISM AND SECOND LANGUAGE ACQUISITION

CHAPTER OUTLINE

INTRODUCTION
GROWING UP BILINGUAL
THEORIES OF SECOND LANGUAGE ACQUISITION
        Foreign educators' contributions
        Child language researchers' contributions
        Linguists' approaches to second language acquisition
        Psycholinguists' approaches to second language processing
        Socio-cultural approaches to second language learning
SUMMARY
        Is there an optimal age for starting second language acquisition?
        How long does it take to learn a second language?
        Are there optimal conditions for the acquisition of a second language?
        What are the characteristics of very good or very poor second language learners?
        To what extent is second language acquisition like first language acquisition in terms of a) stages or intermediate steps; b) underlying acquisition processes; c) predictive or facilitative factors?
        Can learners function as efficiently and competently in communicating, learning, reading, and talking in a second as in a first language?
        To what extent is performance in a second language affected positively or negatively by the structure of the first language?
        To what extent is performance in a first language facilitated or impeded by the acquisition of a second language?

KEY CONCEPTS

A. Although the majority of Americans speak only English, most people in the world are bilingual to some extent. Most people who use more than one language on a daily basis use different languages for different situations.

B. The term *second language acquisition* refers to cases in which a person who already speaks one language is introduced to a second language, either through **submersion, immersion** or in a formal foreign language classroom. If two languages are learned simultaneously from birth, this is referred to as *native bilingualism*.

C. Much of the research on second language acquisition has been motivated by practical questions, such as how to improve foreign language teaching and learning, and how to improve the academic achievement of children who start school unable to speak English. Other researchers have focused on questions about the organization of more than one language in the brain, attempting to discover if language is localized the same way in the brains of bilinguals and monolinguals.

D. Children whose mothers and fathers speak different languages typically grow up bilingual if their parents speak to them consistently in both languages. Bilinguals often produce utterances that contain elements of both languages (**code switches**). In some bilingual communities, code switching for certain items become the norm, and identifies speakers as members of that community.

E. Children who grow up with two languages often display precocious metalinguistic skills since they learn very early on that names for things and ways of expressing ideas are arbitrary and different in different languages. Growing up in a bilingual household does not contribute to or cause language problems or delays.

F. Native bilinguals need to keep speaking both languages if they are to maintain proficiency, since children as well as adults tend to lose languages they don't use often (*language attrition*). Language attrition occurs even faster in children than in adults. Once bilingual children in a monolingual community start attending school and making friends, they may even refuse to speak the less useful language.

G. The best methods of foreign language teaching have been discussed at least since the time of the Roman Empire. Current research on second language teaching has focused on students in foreign language classes. These students typically have noticeable accents, make many errors in grammar, morphology and word choice, and may progress quite slowly.

H. Popular methods of teaching foreign language alternate between *grammar/translation methods* (instruction is in the student's native language, with an emphasis on reading and relatively little conversation) and *direct methods* (instruction is in the second language and teachers avoid stating formal rules). Today, most foreign language teaching involves a mixture of the two methods.

I. Contrastive analysis (analyzing two languages to see where they are different) is used to predict in which areas speakers of one language will have difficulty learning the second language because of *interference errors,* and in which areas they will find the second language easy to learn (positive transfer).

J. One of the difficulties facing foreign language teachers is that there are enormous personal differences in the speed and ultimate attainment of individuals in a language class. Carroll (1981) devised a test of foreign language aptitude (Carroll's Modern Language Aptitude Test) that identified four factors that predict success in foreign language learning:
    1. associative memory
    2. sound-symbol association
    3. inductive ability
    4. grammatical sensitivity

K. Motivation also plays a very important role in second language acquisition. *Integrative motivation* (the desire to identify with the culture of the language being learned) and *instrumental motivation* (the desire to learn the language as a means to and end, such as getting a better job) are both powerful helpers to people who are learning a second language.

L. Research on child language acquisition has contributed to the study of SL acquisition, with particular focus on the similarities and differences between learning a first and a second language.

M. Children moved to a second language setting without explicit instruction tend to make some of the same *developmental errors* as children learning a first language, and will, like very young children, make overgeneralization errors based upon the features of the target language.

N. Second language learners in an untutored situation learn the target language in essentially the same order as first language learners of that language. Speakers from different language backgrounds show similar orders of acquisition and similar errors, which suggests that the target language exerts more influence over acquisition than habits brought over from the native language. Second language learners use identifiable strategies of acquisition that mimic those of first language learners.

O. The quantity of input in the second language is very important in determining the speed of SL acquisition. People learning in a classroom setting who seek out opportunities to converse with a native speaker learn faster than those who do not.

P. Research has shown that students who are allowed to make typical overgeneralization errors and are corrected by their teachers make better and longer lasting progress than students who are pretaught the rule that would preempt the error.

Q. Linguists' approaches to SL acquisition focus on how errors and abilities reveal principles of Universal Grammar. Linguists believe that at every stage of SL acquisition, learners are operating with an organized system of knowledge known as an *interlanguage grammar*.

R. Because many linguists believe that the LAD becomes inaccessible after a critical period, they argue that SL acquisition is necessarily very different from first language acquisition. However, most linguists believe that Universal Grammar is at least partly accessible to the adult SL learner.

S. Linguists differentiate between the universal principles of UG and the parameters which may be more or less irreversibly set in early childhood. Hyams and others have argued that certain parameters such as the null-subject parameter may be easier to switch from "on" to "off" in second language learning, which is why native speakers of Spanish often have persistent difficulties with always remembering to supply a subject pronoun in English, while native English speakers have no such difficulty with dropping the subject pronoun in Spanish.

T. Psycholinguists' approaches to second language learning view SL acquisition as a special sort of information processing in which language learners must learn to parse an auditory stimulus and connect that parsed stimulus into a semantic representation.

U. The fact that skilled SL learners do much better than novice SL learners when learning a novel artificial language supports the hypothesis that SL acquisition is essentially an information processing skill.

V. The **competition model** of sentence processing has been frequently applied to SL acquisition research. According to the competition model, sentence interpretation is governed by accumulated knowledge that certain cues probably indicate certain semantic roles. In SL acquisition, cue strengths are carried over into the early SL learning period. According to this view, the processing tendencies one imports from one's native language can impede SL acquisition.

W. Psycholinguistic processing approaches break down the distinction between comprehension and learning and claim that learning a second language is the same as learning a first language except that one starts with more information. Within a psycholinguistic perspective, there are processing costs for being bilingual, such as a slightly depressed reading speed and increased lexical retrieval time because of the greater amount of information to be dealt with.

X. Socio-cultural approaches focus on the societal context of bilingualism. Socio-cultural researchers point out that language use is closely tied to personal identity and cultural identification and maintain that these issues may actively interfere with second language learning. These approaches also recognize the social nature of language and reject the idea of identifying better or worse varieties of any language in favor of communicative effectiveness and social appropriateness.

MULTIPLE CHOICE QUESTIONS

1. A foreign language class in which the teacher uses only the foreign language when presenting class materials is using which method of instruction?
       a. submersion
*   b. immersion
       c. involvement
       d. survival

(PAGE 393)

2. What specific language skills are often precociously developed in native bilingual children?
       a. semantic awareness
       b. orthographic skills
*   c. metalinguistic skills
       d. grammatical skills

(PAGE 395)

3. Children growing up bilingual
       a. have more language delays and language problems than children growing up in monolingual households
       b. have fewer language delays than children growing up in monolingual households
       c. have language development levels essentially identical to children growing up in monolingual households
*   d. may show vocabulary scores in each language that are slightly depressed in the preschool years

(PAGE 395)

4. When bilingual children go to a monolingual school
*   a. they often begin to display language attrition in the less useful language
     b. they often have difficulty keeping their two languages separate
     c. they tend to feel superior to their monolingual classmates
     d. they often find their knowledge of a second language helps them to learn other language systems such as reading and writing

(PAGE 396)

5. Contrastive analysis would predict that Spanish speakers would have difficulty learning the English form of the possessive because of
     a. transference errors
*   b. interference errors
     c. word order strategies
     d. a different setting of the possessive parameter

(PAGE 398)

6. According to Carroll's Modern Language Aptitude Test (1981), which of these factors contributes to successful foreign language learning?
     a. associative memory and sound-symbol association
     b. inductive ability
     c. grammatical sensitivity
*   d. all of the above

(PAGE 399)

7. Historically, one major difference between the way researchers assessed the progress of children learning a first language and adults learning a second language is that
*   a. children's errors in first language learning were regarded as signs of progress whereas adult errors in second language learning were regarded as signs of failure
     b. child language researchers focused more on the child's acquisition of concepts such as the idea of the past, whereas SL researchers focused more on the appropriate use of the forms
     c. SL learners were expected to learn language at a faster rate than first language users
     d. none of the above

(PAGE 401)

8. Studies of children from different language backgrounds learning English as a second language show that they
     a. use identifiable strategies of acquisition that mimic those of young first language users
     b. avoid transfer of highly marked structures and idiomatic forms from their native language
     c. learn faster if they have no formal instruction
*   d. both a and b

(PAGE 402)

9. An example that a linguist would cite as a "difficult to reset" parameter is
     a. use of possessive pronouns
     b. structure of tag questions
*   c. head direction
     d. conversational rules

(PAGE 404)

10. What is the effect of allowing second language learners to make overgeneralization errors in the target language?
      a. it slows learning of the grammatical rule
*   b. it produces longer lasting learning than preteaching the grammatical rule
      c. it has no effect on learning the grammatical rule
      d. it tends to undermine confidence in SL learners who generally would rather learn to speak correctly as quickly as possible

(PAGE 403)

11. Linguists would argue that adult SL learners need to develop very different learning strategies from first language learners because
*   a. they have passed out of the critical period in which the LAD is accessible to them
      b. they have to reset all of their parameters
      c. they have to explicitly study the Universal Grammar
      d. they have to rely almost entirely on translation rather than on an unmediated language experience

(PAGE 404)

12. According to a linguistic point of view, how would an adult SL learner arrive at proficiency in the grammar of the target language?
*   a. by using a series of interlanguage grammars
      b. by accessing the LASS
      c. by adjustments of his vocabulary choice
      d. he will never achieve proficiency in a second language

(PAGE 404)

13. According to advocates of the psycholinguistic processing approach
      a. learning a second language is easier than learning a first language if one approaches it with the right attitude
      b. second language learners fare better if they spend time abroad
      c. the focus of second language learning should be on learning grammatical rules since performance generally follows competence
*   d. learning a second language is just like learning a first language, except that one starts with more information

(PAGE 406)

14. Sociocultural approaches pay the **least** attention to
      a. social appropriateness
      b. pragmatic use of language
*   c. grammatical correctness
      d. communicative effectiveness

(PAGE 409)

15. According to sociocultural approaches to SL learning, one factor that might keep people from learning a foreign language as well as they could is
      a. a lack of appropriate multilingual role models
*   b. learning a second language might threaten the learner's sense of personal identity
      c. the social rules governing the use of language are often very hard to translate from one language culture to another
      d. because teaching methods are generally very poor

(PAGE 407)

16. According to a sociocultural approach, what might be a good explanation for why Spanish speakers in two way bilingual programs in this country learn English faster than English speakers learn Spanish?
- * a. because Spanish is seen as a stigmatized language
- b. because English is easier to learn than Spanish
- c. because Spanish speaking children generally come from a more intellectually motivated culture
- d. because English speaking teachers have more advanced teaching methods

(PAGE 408)

17. Researchers who adopt a psycholinguistic processing approach to language acquisition argue that interference from a first to a second language is likely to operate
- a. because of competing rules in the first language
- * b. at the level of processing tendencies
- c. because of habits acquired in the first language
- d. because of permanently set parameters

(PAGE 405)

18. Research has shown that
- a. young children learn foreign languages faster than high school aged children and adults, no matter what the teaching method
- * b. in formal classroom instruction, high school aged children and adults learn languages much faster than younger children
- c. in an untutored setting, younger children learn foreign languages faster than adults
- d. the linguist's hypothesis for a critical age for language learning is at least partially supported by the fact that people learning a second language in adulthood almost never attain native-like proficiency

(PAGE 410)

19. What is a possible side effect of learning a second language?
- a. attrition of the first language
- b. heightened metalinguistic skills
- c. enhanced understanding of communicative situations
- * d. all of the above

(PAGE 412)

20. What has proven to be the best method for learning a foreign language?
- a. intensive classroom instruction
- b. total immersion in the foreign culture
- c. becoming personally intimate with a speaker of the foreign language
- * d. different researchers would argue for different methodologies

(PAGE 410)

SHORT ANSWER QUESTIONS

1. Code switching is a frequent phenomenon among bilinguals. Explain this term and give an example.

2. Some researchers have claimed that bilingualism enhances children's metalinguistic skills. What is an example of one such skill?

-77-

3. How might contrastive analysis of languages like Spanish and English be used to improve foreign language teaching, according to researchers in this tradition? Provide an example.

4. Speakers of very different languages like Thai and German make similar errors acquiring English as a second language (e.g., they say *hided* and *foots*). How do bilingualism researchers who are in the child language research tradition explain this?

5. What, according to bilingualism researchers in the linguistic tradition, is an *interlanguage grammar*, and what is the reason for its existence?

6. Researchers in the linguistic tradition are not interested in second language learners' motivation to acquire the second language, nor in their aptitude, vocabulary, or communicative effectiveness. What, then, is the major focus of research for these investigators?

7. In two-way bilingualism programs in the U.S., Spanish speakers learn English faster than English speakers learn Spanish. How do sociocultural researchers explain this?

8. What do adherents of the critical period hypothesis believe about the likelihood that college freshmen can acquire a second language with native-like proficiency?

ESSAY QUESTIONS

1. Discuss the kinds of contributions that the study of second language acquisition can make to linguistic theory.

2. Describe the kinds of factors that may affect the speed of acquisition and ultimate success in a second language that an individual may attain..

3. Some claim that children are better second language learners, while others say that adolescents and adults are better. Discuss the evidence for these conflicting claims.

4. What is the major focus of psycholinguistic research on second language learning, and how does the competition model exemplify this approach?

5. If a friend asked you "How long does it take to learn a second language?", what factors would you emphasize in your response?

APPENDIX ONE: GUIDE TO AUDIOSAMPLES

An audiocassette has been designed to accompany this instructor's manual. It contains materials for classroom demonstration and exercises. The following section provides a guide to these audiosamples, as well as handouts for class use.

We recommend that the tape be played on a portable stereo system ("boombox") for best reception. Additionally, instructors and students should keep in mind that some of these materials (such as the conversational speech excerpts and the synthesized speech continua) were originally meant to be heard over headphones in sound shielded chambers. Thus, responses obtained in classroom exercises are likely to be somewhat variable. It is our hope, however, that these materials will provide instructors and students with a more vivid appreciation of some of the issues discussed in the text than would otherwise be possible.

AUDIOSAMPLES FOR USE WITH CHAPTER TWO:
The Biological Bases of Human Communicative Behavior

<u>APHASIA</u>

The following two speech samples illustrate two major forms of aphasia. One is provided by a Broca's aphasic, while the other was taken from a Wernicke's aphasic. Contrast each sample's grammatical and fluency characteristics.

<u>Patient A (Wernicke's aphasia):</u>

Doctor: You worked in three departments?

Patient: I worked in-in in the same department all the way through, although I was especially you know hanging there for the- for the- and then...um, dear, ordinarily I can I can handle everything, if I could only get things put away for a short while and knock me off I'd be all right. I-I was sure I was going to get another kn- knocked off again this week again for the de- for the dependent, I get another department,... and I haven't done it yet.

Doctor: You mean another operation?

Patient: Yeah, he's supposed to hit me another in the brain and the brain's up here, you see I picked two of them already this week, see? Two weeks, two weeks ago-, one month they gave me the first two weeks, and that was the second week I was working over here, and then the third, uh, the-the third time they hit me was the fourth fourth week I was waiting to hear again, they finished it. And I-I thought it was this week uh coming now. Maybe the next week, the force comes to it and I can't remember now wh-what the other one is, see? They're supposed to come in this one again.

I got it in the- in the- in the brain and they hit him in here and they hit him over here and this one here, I figure the next time they hit this will knock this off [unintelligible]...

Doctor: Knock it off?

Patient: Yeah. The brain's where they come, see? They'll put me asl- can be a soup a bub... Can be about a week, I mean a day, or or a day and uh maybe two or three hours, or...or ... five minutes or ten minutes more. ...they'll put the other bow- bow department on me after they get through...doing it, and they start off, and they take and put about uh I would say eight different or maybe eight...yeah, about nine...nine, ten, about ten ten nouts. Their bones are right across my - one over here and one over here, see and they leave them there. And then the first thing you know they give me a couple more, see? And, oh, maybe it'll be a couple in here, see? And then they give me a couple more, and they'll be up here somewhere, see? And then later on give me a couple more up here...

Patient B (Broca's aphasia):

CLINICIAN: Now, can you tell me a little bit about why you're here in the hospital?

CLIENT: Speech mainly, speech.

CLINICIAN: What happened?

CLIENT: The brain is- see-... headaches ... first.

CLIENT: Headaches all the time.
One month and uh, ... the baby dieds...

CLINICIAN: Your baby?

CLIENT: Yeah...[trIsmɛnts), uh one year ago ... s- Chrismonts day...died.

CLIENT: Uh, one ... week ... later, one week later... myself is ... gone ... (client snaps fingers and makes noise).

CLIENT: The brain ... [sipiz]...the brain seepage. The blood, uh the spinal column is blood.

CLIENT: Operating, and here I am. [laughs]

CLINICIAN: This was when?

CLIENT: Um, March ... one ... year later, yeah!

CLINICIAN: About a year ago?

CLIENT: Yeah, yeah.

CLINICIAN: And, uh, how long have you been in this hospital here?

CLIENT: One, two, three, four months.
Four months.

CLINICIAN: What was the type of work you were doing before you got sick?

CLIENT: Foreman.

CLINICIAN: Foreman?

CLIENT: Yeah.

CLINICIAN: Can you tell me a little bit about that? What you had to do, where it was, and so on?

CLIENT: Sup-tum-vize, supervise ... [rɛkɚz], ... [rɛktərz].

CLINICIAN: Which?

CLIENT: Wreckers...paper.

CLINICIAN: Um hum, <u>records</u>?

CLIENT: Yeah.

(Samples courtesy of Dr. Harold Goodglass)

AUDIOSAMPLE FOR CHAPTER THREE:
Speech Perception

Listening to words taken out of their original context

In the following exercise, you will hear examples of words that have been excised (by a computer waveform editing program) from conversational speech. Although the original conversations were very easy to understand, you will discover that single words are very short acoustic phenomena, and that they are difficult to process out of their original context. You will hear each word three times. Try to guess what word you have heard. Then turn the page to see the answers. This exercise is similar to one carried out by Pollack & Pickett (1963).

1. _____   19. _____
2. _____   20. _____
3. _____   21. _____
4. _____   22. _____
5. _____   23. _____
6. _____   24. _____
7. _____   25. _____
8. _____   26. _____
9. _____   27. _____
10. _____   28. _____
11. _____   29. _____
12. _____   30. _____
13. _____   31. _____
14. _____   32. _____
15. _____   33. _____
16. _____   34. _____
17. _____
18. _____

ANSWER KEY: CONVERSATIONAL SPEECH EXCERPTS

1. like
2. at
3. home
4. box
5. for
6. get
7. phone
8. put
9. hand
10. box
11. tape
12. don't
13. nice
14. stay
15. down
16. there
17. see
18. box
19. toys
20. books
21. doll
22. comb
23. ball
24. have
25. door
26. can
27. go
28. go
29. shoes
30. books
31. can
32. sit
33. floor
34. play

DISCUSSION: These words were taken from a conversation between a mother and her one-year old child. Would this **context** have helped you to identify more words? Are there indications that these words came from **child-directed speech**? Some words do not sound like words at all, just rather fast noise bursts. Consonants with very short embedded vowels (<50 msec.) tend to create this impression. At the ends of utterances, speakers often fall into **glottal fry**, which is very low pitched and slow glottal pulsing. Can you identify any words which probably came from the ends of utterances? Discuss differences between the intelligibility of **content words** and **function words**.

AUDIOSAMPLE FOR CHAPTER THREE: SPEECH PERCEPTION

IDENTIFICATION AND DISCRIMINATION OF VOICE ONSET TIME (VOT)

For the instructor:

Seven synthetic speech syllables were generated at the Haskins Laboratories, New Haven, Conn. The syllables are CVs in which the first syllable is a bilabial stop consonant and the vowel is [a]. The syllables differ in voice-onset-time (VOT) ranging from zero to 60 msec voicing lag. Zero VOT means that the release of air pressure and the onset of voicing was simultaneous; 60 msec voicing lag means that there was a 60 msec interval between the burst and the onset of voicing. The stimuli are perceived as either a [ba] or a [pa]. For monolingual American English speakers, stimuli with VOTs between zero and 20 msec voicing lag are perceived as [ba]; those with VOTs of 40 to 60 msec voicing lag are perceived as [pa]. The stimulus with a 30 msec voicing lag may be heard as [ba] or [pa]. Most probably it will constitute the cross-over stimulus.

The taped material consists of two parts: (1) **A 7-step voicing continuum.** The 7 stimuli are played sequentially, starting with zero VOT and ending with 60 msec voicing lag in VOT. (2) **An Identification Test** consisting of 5 different randomizations of the 7 stimuli in the continuum.

After the class has listened to the tapes and marked the answer sheets, you may use the VOT values provided in the transcript of the **Identification Test** to help you note, on the answer sheet, the VOT value of each stimulus. Write in the appropriate cell, in the table below, the listener's response to each presentation of the 7 stimuli.

Stimulus VOT	1	2	3	4	5	total b	total p	% b	% p
0									
10									
20									
30									
40									
50									
60									

FOR THE INSTRUCTOR: DESCRIPTION OF THE SYNTHESIZED SPEECH
SPEECH STIMULI

1. **Demonstration of a 7-step Voicing continuum** going from [ba] to [pa]. The numerical values represent VOT in msec. The tape contains the CV syllables and does not contain the number of the trial.

1. 0
2. 10
3. 20
4. 30
5. 40
5. 50
7. 60

2. **Identification Test** with five randomizations of the VOT values in msec. The tape contains the CV syllables grouped in blocks of 7 trials. There is a longer interval between the blocks than between individual trials.

1. 30	22. 60
2. 0	23. 50
3. 40	24. 40
4. 10	25. 10
5. 40	26. 20
6. 30	27. 0
7. 50	28. 20
8. 0	29. 30
9. 60	30. 60
10. 30	31. 50
11. 50	32. 60
12. 20	33. 30
13. 10	34. 40
14. 20	35. 10
15. 20	
16. 50	
17. 40	
18. 0	
19. 10	
20. 60	
21. 0	

ANSWER SHEET: IDENTIFICATION AND DISCRIMINATION OF VOT

1. Practice trials using the **7-step voicing continuum**: For each stimulus, indicate whether it sounds like [ba] or [pa].

1. ba   pa
2. ba   pa
3. ba   pa
4. ba   pa
5. ba   pa
6. ba   pa
7. ba   pa

2. **Identification test**: For each stimulus indicate whether it sounds like [ba] or [pa]

1. ba   pa
2. ba   pa
3. ba   pa
4. ba   pa
5. ba   pa
6. ba   pa
7. ba   pa

8. ba   pa
9. ba   pa
10. ba   pa
11. ba   pa
12. ba   pa
13. ba   pa
14. ba   pa

15. ba   pa
16. ba   pa
17. ba   pa
18. ba   pa
19. ba   pa
20. ba   pa
21. ba   pa

22. ba   pa
23. ba   pa
24. ba   pa
25. ba   pa
26. ba   pa
27. ba   pa
28. ba   pa

29. ba   pa
30. ba   pa
31. ba   pa
32. ba   pa
33. ba   pa
34. ba   pa
35. ba   pa

EXERCISE FOR CHAPTER FIVE

MEMORY FOR SENTENCES

For the instructor:

The following pages provide two passages and sets of related sentences used in Sachs, J. "Memory in reading and listening to discourse," Memory and Cognition, 1974, 2, 95-100. These passages and several others had been used in Sachs, J., "Recognition memory for syntactic and semantic aspects of connected discourse," Perception and Psychophysics, 1967, 2, 437-442. The lexical change condition was not used in the 1967 study. The passages were written by the author, based on children's stories, folklore, and simple passages found in newspapers. For further information contact J. Sachs, U-85, University of Connecticut, Storrs, Ct 06268.

In Sach's 1974 study, subjects read paragraphs in which target sentences were embedded. Either immediately after the target sentence, or 20, 40 or 80 syllables later, subjects were asked to indicate whether a probe sentence they read was identical to one in the previously read text.

The following exercise is an adaptation of Sach's original paradigm, which varied passage length and presented subjects with single sentences for recognition judgements. We suggest that you carry out this classroom exercise in the following way: Cut out copies of the four stories. Fold them in the middle to hide the probe sentences and distribute them to the class. Have the students read passage silently and at their own pace. When they finish reading, have them turn the folded page over, and select the sentence they believe was in the paragraph they just read. An answer sheet following the exercise indicates what types of errors were made if the student selected a sentence which did not appear in the paragraph. Sach's findings suggested that, in written materials, meaning was generally preserved over form, although changes from the active to passive voice were surprisingly well detected. At the passage lengths chosen here, subjects were very likely to make errors in recognizing the original form of sentences.

The sentences listed below the passages are related to the underlined sentence in the following ways: I = identical; S = semantic change; P = change from active to passive or passive to active; F = formal change; L = lexical change.

After the exercise: Discuss the implications of such results for every day tasks such as mastering lecture materials and readings. The original wording of sentences you read and hear is lost very rapidly; only their meaning is maintained in long-term memory. How might this affect study strategies?

DIRECTIONS FOR READING TASK

<u>Directions: Read this passage at a comfortable reading rate. When you have finished, immediately turn the folded page over and read the five sentences on the other side. Mark the sentence which is **identical** to one in the preceding passage.</u> Do not reread the passage.

<u>Story 1:</u> When Heinrich Schliemann was a little boy his father told him the story of Troy. He liked that story better than anything he had ever heard, and made up his mind that as soon as he could, he would travel to Greece and find Troy. As a matter of fact, when he grew up he did manage to gather a fortune in a short time and equipped an expedition to the northwest corner of Asia Minor. There was a mound that according to tradition has been the home of Prianus, the King of Troy. Schliemann, whose enthusiasm was somewhat greater than his knowledge wasted no time in preliminary explorations, but began at once to dig. Then something curious happened. Instead of finding polished tools and crude pottery, he found statuettes and jewelry. He had dug with such haste and zeal that his trench went straight through the heart of the city for which he was looking and carried him to ruins of another

---
fold the page here before distributing

Which of these sentences appeared in the paragraph you just read?

    ___ Instead of finding statuettes and jewelry, he found polished tools and crude pottery.
    ___ Instead of finding polished tools and crude pottery, he found statuettes and jewelry.
    ___ Instead of finding polished tools and rough pottery, he found statuettes and jewelry.
    ___ Instead of polished tools and crude pottery, statuettes and jewelry were found.
    ___ He found statuettes and jewelry instead of polished tools and crude pottery.

DIRECTIONS FOR READING TASK

<u>Directions</u>: Read this passage at a comfortable reading rate. When you have finished, immediately turn the page over and read the five sentences on the other side. Mark the sentence which is **identical** to one in the preceding passage. Do not reread the passage.

<u>Story 2:</u> Back in 1895 the brothers Lumiere made a thirty-second movie in which a gardener is shown watering a lawn with a hose: A child steps on the hose, the gardener looks into the nozzle to see what has happened, the child steps of, and the gardener gets it full in the fact. That burst of water signalled the marriage of the motion-picture industry to the ancient art of slapstick. The new form went through various stages of development, concentrating in turn on fast one-shot gags, on trick photography, on faster and more improbable action, and finally on combining these elements with the carefully constructed gag running up to five minutes. After they had worked out the basic techniques of film slapstick, its development grew along two separate lines. Mack Sennett went in for more Keystone Cops, more bathing beauties, funnier looking comedians, and faster, broader, more hair-raising action. Chaplin, turning to stories that were more than just a framework to hand gags on, developed characters capable of moving an audience to tears and sympathy as well as laughter.

----
fold the page here before distributing

Which of these sentences appeared in the paragraph you just read?

    ___   After they had worked out the basic techniques of film slapstick,   its development grew along three separate lines.

    ___   After the basic techniques of film slapstick had been worked out, its development grew along two separate lines.

    ___   After they had worked out the basic techniques of film slapstick, it developed along two separate lines.

    ___   After they had worked out the basic techniques of film slapstick, its development grew along two different lines.

    ___   After they had worked out the basic techniques of film slapstick, its development grew along two separate lines.

INSTRUCTOR'S ANSWER SHEET: MEMORY FOR SENTENCES IN TEXT

The sentences listed below the passages are related to the underlined sentence in the following ways: I = identical; S = semantic change; P = change from active to passive or passive to active; F = formal change; L = lexical change.

Story 1:

- S. Instead of finding statuettes and jewelry, he found polished tools and crude pottery.
- P. Instead of polished tools and crude pottery, statuettes and jewelry were found.
- I. Instead of finding polished tools and crude pottery, he found statuettes and jewelry.
- F. He found statuettes and jewelry instead of polished tools and crude pottery.
- L. Instead of finding polished tools and rough pottery, he found statuettes and jewelry.

Story 2:

- S. After they had worked out the basic techniques of film slapstick, its development grew along three separate lines.
- P. After the basic techniques of film slapstick had been worked out, its development grew along two separate lines.
- F. After they had worked out the basic techniques of film slapstick, it developed along two separate lines.
- L. After they had worked out the basic techniques of film slapstick, its development grew along two <u>different</u> lines.
- I. After they had worked out the basic techniques of film slapstick, its development grew along two separate lines.

AUDIOSAMPLE FOR CHAPTER SEVEN: SPEECH PRODUCTION

As the chapter discusses, conversational speech is not very fluent. Have students listen to the speech sample on the tape. What kinds of disfluencies are typical of normal speech production?

CONVERSATIONAL SAMPLE

INTERVIEWER: (And what do you think his top priority should be this year as President?)

SPEAKER: *Uh*, the economy. I think if *uh* the-- I think if you solve a lot of the *uh* economic problems you'll solve a lot of other problems, *you know uh... you know*, when economics or <when the>-- when people are out of work, don't have money, crime goes up, drug use goes up. *Uh*, I think you have, *you know*, a psychological type of disorders go up... *You know*, people become a little bit... anxious, and I think... if you solve that-- <if you can help rel-- uh, resolve that problem>... *I mean* you'll help solve a lot of other problems. *You know, we-we* won't be as tight with other people. I-- n- *not* not tight, *tight* in the sense of money, *you know-- you... you know*, people are... right now, *you know* "why give money to this country-- why do this *you know* for these people--why do this for that". And *you know*... <I it's>-- *the reason is* because they don't have a job or they're afraid they'll lose their job and there won't be money for them if <they have to collect or>... *you know that that* type of *uh* anxiety.

INTERVIEWER: (What do you think he should do to take over what President Bush has started in Somalia?)

SPEAKER: I think he ought to take the weapons away from those people... I mean... I-if you go in and people put their faith in you like you're gonna straighten it out...*um...and uh...* and people feel like they-- *you know* <they're>... I guess *if if*-- let's say you lived in a neighborhood and there were people that were in the neighborhood that were... *um* trying to control it-- *you know* or *uh* antagonize everybody... and the police came in... and... just stood there, *and and* then *you know, uh w-what* good have you done? *Uh* they're gonna take it out on the people who are still there, not the people who have left... So if these people aren't somehow... *you know* disarmed and... they're not... *uh* encouraged or... *you know have have* some sort of a... reason to work together, then I think when the-- *when the* Americans or the U.N. leaves or whatever, *it's it's* gonna be just as bad if not worse... *So so*-- I don't know. I think you've got to get a process rolling over there. It doesn't seem like there's *you know* anybody who's elected or... takes over doesn't seem to have a real chance... *Uh... didn't didn't* the leader there leave or something like that--just bolt? 'Cause *you know* you got a bunch of gangs running the country? I don't know.

DISCUSSION AND ACTIVITIES FOR CHAPTER SEVEN

The speaker on the audiosample for Chapter Seven seems very disfluent, but demonstrates a very typical profile of conversational speech. Formulating responses to difficult questions is likely to result in large numbers of pauses, fillers and "mazes" (utterance segments which seem to lead nowhere and are dropped or revised).

Are the disfluencies randomly distributed? Discuss how the location of disfluencies suggests something about the sentence formulation process.

Discuss speaking environments which are more and less likely to be characterized by large numbers of speech disfluencies. Test your hypotheses by listening carefully to speakers engaged in various types of verbal interactions.

AUDIOSAMPLES FOR CHAPTER EIGHT: LANGUAGE DEVELOPMENT

"ADAMI LEARNS TO TALK"

The audiosample for Chapter Eight follows a single child's language development over a three year span, and consists of 8 samples of interactions between the child and his mother and other adults. These samples were obtained during naturalistic play and bookreading interactions carried out at the child's bedtime each night; some extraneous household noise can be heard on some of the samples.

As the first sample will indicate, the child, Adami, was a somewhat slow language learner. His first sample at age 1;9 (years;months) shows only simple single word utterances. The second sample shows a small array of single word, two word and three word utterances, as well as minor usage of grammatical inflections, such as the plural. Subsequent samples show increased length of utterance, greater usage of grammatical inflections and increasing conversational competence. By the final tapings at ages 3;2 and 4;6, Adami is able to carry on a conversation with a stranger about events which took place in the past, such as receiving a toy. The tapes illustrate the rapidity with which children move from single words to complex grammar.

The transcripts on the following pages which accompany the taped excerpts follow transcript conventions described in B. MacWhinney (1991) (The CHILDES project: Tools for analyzing talk. (Hillsdale, NJ: LEA)) for data in the CHILDES archive, and for use with CLAN language analysis programs. Adami's non-adult pronunciation is written in Unibet, a computer phonetic transcription system, under each of his utterances on lines which are prefaced by the string %pho. Unintelligible utterances by adults and the child are transcribed as **xxx**.

Discussion topics:

    1. Describe changes in the child's use of vocabulary, grammar, and conversational adequacy over the course of the taped interactions.

    2. These tapes also illustrate **child-directed speech** and how it changes over the course of language development. Discuss some of the conversational adjustments made when adults speak to very young children and how this register changes as adults address older children.

    3. Compute Adami's Mean Length of Utterance (MLU) over the eight samples. Discuss changes. How does adult MLU change as Adami's language matures?

```
@Begin
@Participants:   CHI Adami child, MOT Mother
@Age of CHI:     1;9.
@Date:   6-OCT-1989
@Coder:  Becky Rooney
*MOT:   did you find the zipper?
*MOT:   can you pull it?
*MOT:   should mama help you?
*MOT:   here pull the zipper.
*MOT:   here it is.
*MOT:   pull the zipper.
*MOT:   there you go.
*MOT:   what did you do?
*CHI:   xxx.
*MOT:   what's the matter?
*CHI:   xxx.
*MOT:   hmm?
*MOT:   it's all finished.
*MOT:   we zipped it all the way up.
*MOT:   is it all finished?
*MOT:   it's all finished yeah.
*MOT:   ok.
*CHI:   xxx.
*MOT:   should we pick a book?
*CHI:   xxx.
*MOT:   alright what book should we pick?
*MOT:   you tell mama what book?
*MOT:   what book should we do?
*MOT:   hmm?
*MOT:   let's take the xxx.
*MOT:   what book should we do?
*CHI:   xxx.
*MOT:   should we do hop on Pop?
*CHI:   xxx.
*MOT:   hmm what book should we do?
*MOT:   can we do this one?
*MOT:   what is that?
*CHI:   hop.
%pho:   ba.
*CHI:   hop$hop.
%pho:   ba$ba.
*MOT:   hop on Pop?
*MOT:   ok.
*MOT:   should we do this one?
*CHI:   three.
%pho:   gi.
*MOT:   we should do three books?
*CHI:   xxx.
*MOT:   well what book is this?
*MOT:   should we do this book?
*CHI:   xxx.
*MOT:   should we # what book should we do first?
*CHI:   these.
%pho:   gi.
*MOT:   these two?
```

```
*CHI:   xxx.
*MOT:   ok these two.
*MOT:   hmm what's this?
*CHI:   xxx.
*MOT:   hmm?
*CHI:   xxx.
*MOT:   is that your new shoe?
*CHI:   xxx.
*MOT:   got some new shoes hmmn?
*MOT:   ok should we put this book down first?
*MOT:   we'll put it right here.
*MOT:   ok this is a book called+...
*CHI:   hop$hop$hop.
%pho:   ba$ba$ba.
*MOT:   hop on Pop that's right.
*CHI:   hop$hop$hop.
%pho:   ba$ba$ba.
*MOT:   pup up pup is # what?
*MOT:   pup is # up.
*MOT:   what is this one?
*MOT:   cup cup +/.
*CHI:   xxx pup pup pup.
%pho:   xxx ba ba bup.
*MOT:   pup in+...
*CHI:   no.
%pho:   no.
*MOT:   cup.
*CHI:   xxx.
*MOT:   cup+/.
*CHI:   xxx.
*MOT:   cup cup on+/.
*CHI:   xxx.
*MOT:   cup.
*MOT:   what's this?
*CHI:   xxx.
%pho:   no no rE rE.
*MOT:   i can't tell with your fingers in your mouth+/.
*CHI:   xxx.
*MOT:   what is this?
*MOT:   what is this?
*MOT:   xxx.
*MOT:   what?
*MOT:   what?
*CHI:   [=! drinks something].
*MOT:   oh always drinking.
*MOT:   mouse house.
*MOT:   mouse on+...
*MOT:   mouse on+...
*CHI:   xxx.
*MOT:   mouse on what?
*MOT:   what's this?
*MOT:   what's this?
*MOT:   can you tell me?
@End
```

```
@Begin
@Participants:   CHI Adami child, MOT Mother
@Age of CHI:     2;3.
@Date:  6-MAY-1990
@Coder: Becky Rooney
*MOT:   what else is # what else did Cheryl put in this book?
*CHI:   Car.
%pho:   ka.
*MOT:   a car.
*MOT:   and what's that?
*CHI:   that's +/.
*MOT:   what are those+/.
*CHI:   machine machine machine machine.
%pho:   du Sin Sin Sin.
*MOT:   machine machine machine.
*MOT:   how many machines?
*CHI:   three nine two.
%pho:   di nAn tu.
*CHI:   two xxx &t two.
%pho:   tu mAs &t tu.
*MOT:   two?
*CHI:   yes two.
%pho:   nEs tu.
*MOT:   i think it's one two+...
*CHI:   three.
%pho:   vi.
*MOT:   three+...
*CHI:   machine-s.
%pho:   Sinz.
*MOT:   that's right three machines.
*MOT:   and what is this?
*MOT:   hmm hmm are you drinking your juice?
*CHI:   machine.
%pho:   Sin.
*MOT:   that's not a machine.
*MOT:   what is that?
*CHI:   xxx boat.
%pho:   &s bot.
*MOT:   that's not a boat.
*MOT:   what is that?
*CHI:   machine.
%pho:   Sin.
*MOT:   that's a train.
*CHI:   train.
%pho:   tSen.
*MOT:   yeah you have that same train don't you?
*CHI:   out.
%pho:   aut.
*MOT:   yours is outside that's right.
*CHI:   no see.
%pho:   no si.
*MOT:   you don't+...
*MOT:   you haven't seen it?
*CHI:   no.
%pho:   no.
```

```
*MOT:	it's on the patio.
*CHI:	oh.
%pho:	o.
*MOT:	you xxx in pieces.
*CHI:	[=! laughs].
*MOT:	[=! laughs].
%com:	(Break in tape).
*MOT:	tonight Adam's really tired.
*CHI:	[=! cries].
*MOT:	yeah # let's+...
*MOT:	alright now.
*CHI:	me see.
%pho:	mi si.
*CHI:	&n mom me see.
%pho:	&n mam ni si.
*MOT:	well +/.
*CHI:	no me # see.
%pho:	no ni # si.
*MOT:	you haven't seen your train recently?
*CHI:	nuhuh.
%pho:	6 A
*MOT:	it's outside.
*MOT:	it's in the backyard.
*CHI:	nuhuh.
%pho:	n6 A.
*MOT:	it is.
*CHI:	no.
%pho:	no.
*MOT:	should we look out the window and see it?
*CHI:	hmm.
*MOT:	it's there.
@End



@Begin
@Participants:	CHI Adami child, MOT Mother
@Age of CHI:	2;7.
@Date: 6-SEP-1990
@Coder: Becky Rooney
*MOT:	homework?
*MOT:	did you bring any homework?
*CHI:	nuhuh.
%pho:	n6 A.
*MOT:	i don't think you brought any homework with you.
*CHI:	uhuh.
%pho:	A 6.
*MOT:	what are we going to bring for sharing time this week?
*CHI:	um # my doctor kit too.
%pho:	Am # mi dak dak dIng tu.
*MOT:	well you already brought your doctor kit.
*CHI:	again.
%pho:	dEn.
*MOT:	no you can't bring it again.
*MOT:	you have to bring something different.
*MOT:	maybe we should bring the bug downstairs.
*CHI:	huh?
%pho:	hA?
```

```
*MOT:	maybe we should bring what we caught this morning.
*CHI:	xxx.
*MOT:	what would # what should we bring?
*CHI:	no xxx bag.
%pho:	no xxx d&g.
*MOT:	what?
*CHI:	no bag # show it.
%pho:	no d&g # So It.
*MOT:	there's no bag to show it in?
*CHI:	uh uh.
%pho:	A 6.
*MOT:	well should +/.
*CHI:	need bag in it.
%pho:	nid d&g In It.
*MOT:	oh you need to put it in a bag?
*MOT:	you could bring the bug bottle.
*CHI:	uh uh.
%pho:	A 6.
*MOT:	you can't bring the cricket in the bug bottle?
*CHI:	uh uh.
%pho:	A 6.
*MOT:	why not?
*CHI:	cause in bug bottle.
%pho:	traiz A A In 6 Its In d&g baba.
*MOT:	what?
*CHI:	and take that out # && and then and xxx and this xxx up high xxx.
%pho:	&nd tek D&t aut # & &nd DEn &nd A dZA d&g &nd DIs p6kEt opEn xxx
	p6kEt &nd n n ni so hold It der d& 6p hai 6n d&g.
*MOT:	you know something?
*CHI:	huh?
%pho:	hA?
*MOT:	i don't understand a word of it.
*CHI:	xxx.
*MOT:	[=! laughs].
*CHI:	me get up high up there and and something and chair and then
	get the the that out up there and +/.
%pho:	mi gEt Ap 6hai Ap Der &nd &nd sompIN &nd tSe &nd dEn gEt dA dA
	d&t aut Ap der &nd +/.
*MOT:	get your bag out up there yeah.
*CHI:	up there.
%pho:	Ap Der.
*MOT:	yeah.
*CHI:	see # me pointing up there.
%pho:	si # mi pOintIN Ap ser.
*MOT:	i see you're pointing up there but what's up there?
*CHI:	bag-s.
%pho:	Ad&gz.
*MOT:	bags # what kind of bags?
*CHI:	um uh uh um supermarket one-s.
%pho:	Am A A Am sup3markEt wAnz.
*MOT:	supermarket ones?
*CHI:	uhhuh.
%pho:	AhA.
*MOT:	supermarket bags.
*MOT:	well don't you think we could just leave the cricket in the in the
	bottle and bring the bottle to school?
```

-99-

```
*CHI:	um the bottle in bag and then xxx.
%pho:	Am dE badE In d&g &nd den ba.
*MOT:	we could put the bottle in the bag?
*CHI:	uhhuh.
%pho:	A.
@End


@Begin
@Participants:	CHI Adami Child, Mot Mother
@Age of CHI:	2;8.
@Date: 6-OCT-1990
@Coder: Becky Rooney
*MOT:	ok should we read this book?
*CHI:	um this hard book read.
%pho:	Am dIs ha3 bUk rid.
*MOT:	why is it a hard book to read?
*CHI:	it-'s just big.
%pho:	Its dZAs bI.
*MOT:	oh because it's so big.
*CHI:	yes.
%pho:	nEs.
*MOT:	ok but you know the story.
*CHI:	yes.
%pho:	nEs.
*MOT:	it's called # Goldi +...
*CHI:	locks.
%pho:	naks.
*MOT:	and the +...
*CHI:	and three bear-s.
%pho:	&nd vri b&.
*MOT:	goldilocks and the three bears.
*MOT:	once upon a time there were +...
*CHI:	three bear-s and and that-'s stick-y.
%pho:	fri b&z &nd &nd dAz sIki.
*MOT:	that's sticky?
*MOT:	we'll wipe it.
*MOT:	who lived in a # cottage in the +...
*CHI:	wood-s.
%pho:	wAz.
*MOT:	very # very good.
*MOT:	in the woods.
*CHI:	clock.
%pho:	trak.
*MOT:	that's a clock.
*MOT:	that's right.
*MOT:	and each morning at breakfast the papa bear sat in his great +...
*CHI:	big chair.
%pho:	bIg tSe.
*MOT:	and the mama bear sat in her middle # sized chair +/.
*CHI:	chair.
%pho:	tSe.
*MOT:	and the baby bear sat in his +...
*CHI:	teeny teeny chair.
%pho:	tini tini tS&6.
*MOT:	his teeny teeny chair.
*MOT:	and mama bear cooked delicious +...
*CHI:	porridge.
```

```
%pho:		padZ.
*MOT:		hmm?
*CHI:		porridge.
%pho:		pa3dZ.
*MOT:		porridge # right.
*MOT:		and spooned it into +...
*CHI:		three bowl-s.
%pho:		tri bOz.
*MOT:		right # just the right size for the three # bears.
*CHI:		bear-s.
%pho:		b&z.
*MOT:		but one morning papa bear tasted his first spoonful of porridge and
		said # what +...
*CHI:		too hot!
%pho:		tu hat!
*MOT:		right # and when baby bear tasted his porridge he cried +...
*CHI:		too hot!
%pho:		tu hat!
*MOT:		much too hot # much too hot!
*MOT:		and mama bear felt +...
*CHI:		terrible.
%pho:		tErba:$a.
*MOT:		[=! laughs].
*MOT:		terrible.
@End


@Begin
@Participants:	CHI Adami child, MOT Mother
@Age of CHI:	2;11.
@Date: 6-JAN-1991
@Coder: Becky Rooney
*MOT:		do you know how to drive a truck?
*CHI:		no way!
%pho:		no we!
*MOT:		no way?
*CHI:		no.
%pho:		no.
*CHI:		oh me get big ni grow up me mailman?
%pho:		o ni dEt bIg 6n ro Ap ni melm&n?
*MOT:		when you grow up and get big can you be a mailman?
*MOT:		i don't see why not I suppose you can.
*MOT:		will you bring me the mail?
*MOT:		you would bring me mail?
*MOT:		how many letters?
*CHI:		lots.
%pho:		nats.
*MOT:		lots of letters?
%com:		dog interrupts them.
*CHI:		me take some my &m &m my big big big bag.
%pho:		ni tek sAm mai m6 m6 mai bIg bIg bIg b&g.
*MOT:		you're gonna bring them in your big big big bag?
*MOT:		are you going to be a driving mailman or a walking mailman?
*CHI:		walk-ing.
%pho:		wOkIN.
*MOT:		you would like to walk to deliver the mail?
*CHI:		yes.
%pho:		nEs.
```

```
*CHI:    me bring my truck.
%pho:    ni dIN mai trAk.
*MOT:    you will bring a truck too?
*MOT:    that will help I think.
*CHI:    me bring soda truck.
%pho:    ni dIN sod6 trAk.
*MOT:    you'll drive in a soda truck?
*MOT:    you know dogs bark at mailmen.
*MOT:    what will you do when dogs bark at you?
*CHI:    no me come in.
%pho:    no ni kAm In.
*MOT:    you won't come in?
*CHI:    no.
%pho:    no.
*MOT:    but the dogs will still bark.
*CHI:    mama take it.
%pho:    mam6 tek It.
*MOT:    mam take what?
*CHI:    oh that out my hand-s.
%pho:    o d&t au mai h&nds.
*MOT:    mama will take the mail out of your hands?
*CHI:    yes.
%pho:    nEs.
*MOT:    that way the dogs can't hurt you?
*CHI:    no.
%pho:    no.
@End




@Begin
@Participants:  CHI Adami Child, MOT Mother
@Sex of DWN:    Male
@Age of DWN:    3;2.
@Date: 14-FEB-1991
@Coder: Kim Banson
*CHI:    mama you know &n &n Lance bring(-ed) lots of candy and Lissa &e
         and everybody bring(-ed) lots of candy &a and cookie-s &i (and)
         it make me sick!
%pho:    Es en mama yu no n&ns bwIN nats O k&ndi En nIs6 &nd Evibadi bwIN
         nats O kandi En kUkiz d& nek mi sIk!
*MOT:    they brought lots of candy and cookies and it made you sick?
*CHI:    yes.
%pho:    jEs.
*MOT:    what did we bring?
*CHI:    we bring(-ed) those that we eat(-ed) already.
%pho:    wi briN doz ni it orEdi.
*MOT:    you brought those things that we ate already?
*MOT:    we brought the cake didn't we?
*CHI:    everyone lik-ed those.
%pho:    Eviw6n naIkt doz.
*MOT:    everyone liked those?
@End
```

```
@Begin
@Participants:    CHI Adami Child, KIM Family_Friend, MOT Mother
@Sex of CHI:      Male
@Age of CHI:      3;11.
@Date: 23-NOV-1991
@Coder: Becky Rooney
*KIM:   are these xxx?
*CHI:   you know my mom go&ed on a trip and she come back # she give me
        a a redskin hat and redskin ball.
%pho:   ju no mai mam wEnt an A trIp &nd Si kAm b&k # Si gIv mi A A rEd
        skIn h&t &nd rEd skIn bOl.
*KIM:   a redskin hat and a redskin ball?
*CHI:   uhhuh.
%pho:   6hA.
*KIM:   a football?
*CHI:   no # redskin ball.
%pho:   no # rEdskIn bOl.
*KIM:   what's a redskin ball?
*CHI:   um um my dad has one now I got one.
%pho:   Am Am mai d&d h&z wAn nau ai gat wAn.
*KIM:   wow # you have one just like your dad # that's great.
*CHI:   but it-'s a little bigg-er.
%pho:   bAt Its e lItl bIg6.
*KIM:   a li +/.
%com:   later that day.
*CHI:   Animal-s.
%pho:   &m6lz.
*MOT:   this cord is for animals?
*CHI:   no that corn we get&ed there.
%pho:   no dat korn wi gat der.
*MOT:   oh the corn is for animals.
*CHI:   uhhuh.
%pho:   6hA.
*CHI:   you ca-'nt eat it.
%pho:   ju k&nt it It.
*MOT:   we can't eat it?
*CHI:   no.
%pho:   no.
*CHI:   or cook it.
%pho:   or kUk It.
*MOT:   we can't # we can't cook it # no # or cook it xxx.
*CHI:   it-'s yuck.
%pho:   Its jAk.
*MOT:   yucky corn.
*CHI:   yeah.
%pho:   j&.
*MOT:   well then why will the animals eat it?
*CHI:   cause cause # maybe pumpkin-s can eat it.
%pho:   kAz kAz # mebi p6mpkInz k&n it It.
*MOT:   [=! laughs].
*CHI:   [=! laughs].
*MOT:   maybe the pumpkin will eat it.
@End
```

-103-

```
@Begin
@Participants:   CHI Adami child, AMY Family_Friend
@Sex of CHI:     Male
@Age of CHI:     4;6.
@Date:  1-JUN-1992
@Coder: Becky Rooney
*AMY:   we can play.
*CHI:   I get&ed batman.
%pho:   ai gat b&tm&n.
*AMY:   you have batman?
*AMY:   where's your batman?
*CHI:   I leave&ed him at home.
%pho:   ai lEft hIm &t hom.
*AMY:   you left him at home?
*CHI:   I even have the batman um mobile but it-'s a toy and i get&ed it from
        burger king.
%pho:   ai ivIn h&v d6 b&tm&n um mobil bAt Its e toi &nd ai gat It frAm
        b3g3 kIN.
*AMY:   you did!
*CHI:   and there-'s a button and you push it and then something shoot-s out of
        it.
%pho:   &nd de3z e bUt6n &nd ju pUS It &nd dEn s6mdIN Suts aut Av It.
*AMY:   it shoots out of batman?
*AMY:   what shoots out of batman?
*CHI:   no # out of the mobile.
%pho:   no # aut Av di mobil.
*AMY:   oh # out of the batmobile!
*AMY:   what does he do in the batmobile # does he fly?
*CHI:   um # no it-'s just it-'s just a toy.
%pho:   Am # no Its dZAst Its dZAst e toi.
*AMY:   oh it's just a toy.
@End
```

APPENDIX TWO: OVERHEAD MASTERS

The following pages may be used to create class handouts or overhead transparencies for classroom usage.

This is a Wug.

Now there is another one.
There are two of them.
There are two _ _ _ _.

This is a man who knows how to Naz.
He is Nazzing. He does it every day.
Every day he _ _ _ _ _ _.

This is a man who knows how to Rick.
He is Ricking. He did the same thing
yesterday. What did he do yesterday?
Yesterday he _ _ _ _ _ _.

Copyright © 1993 by Harcourt Brace & Company. All rights reserved.

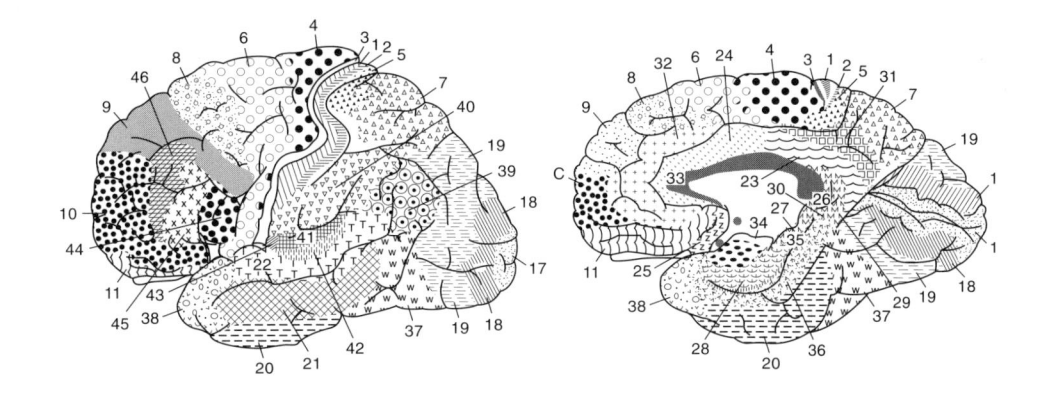

BRODMANN AREA	ANATOMICAL LOCATION	FUNCTION
1, 2, 3	Postcentral gyrus	Primary sensori-motor area (Sm I)
4	Precentral gyrus	Primary motor-sensory area (Ms I)
6	Premotor cortex	Premotor area supplementary motor area (on medial surface) (Ms II)
8	Caudal part of middle frontal gyrus	Frontal eye field
9, 10, 11	Superior, middle and inferior frontal gyri	Judgment, foresight, mood
17	Walls of calcarine sulcus	Primary visual area
18, 19	Occipital lobe	Visual association areas
39	Angular gyrus	Reading and writing (dominant hemisphere)
40	Supramarginal gyrus	Repetition (possibly due to disruption of arcuate fasciculus) (dominant hemisphere)
41	Heschl's gyrus	Primary auditory area
42	Belt of cortex surrounding Heschl's gyrus	Auditory association area
22	Superior temporal gyrus	Posterior third = Wernicke's area (dominant hemisphere)
44, 45	Third frontal gyrus (pars opercularis and triangularis)	Broca's area (dominant hemisphere)

Copyright © 1993 by Harcourt Brace & Company. All rights reserved.

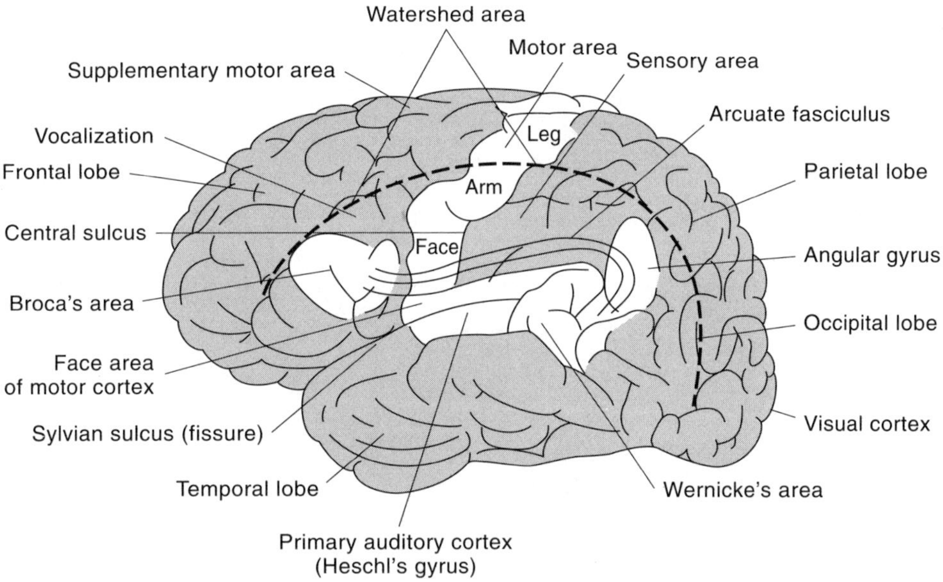
Watershed area
Motor area
Sensory area
Supplementary motor area
Arcuate fasciculus
Vocalization
Leg
Frontal lobe
Arm
Parietal lobe
Central sulcus
Face
Angular gyrus
Broca's area
Occipital lobe
Face area
of motor cortex
Sylvian sulcus (fissure)
Visual cortex
Temporal lobe
Wernicke's area
Primary auditory cortex
(Heschl's gyrus)

(a) (b) (c)

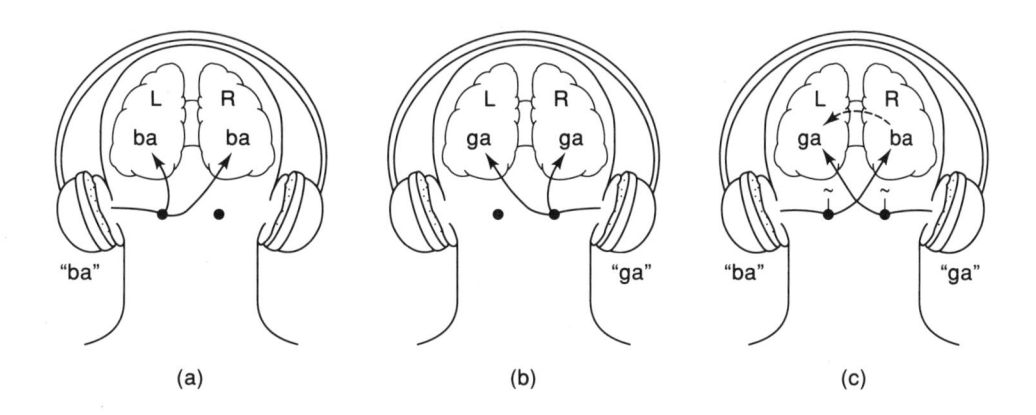

Copyright © 1993 by Harcourt Brace & Company. All rights reserved.

		Place of articulation					
		Bilabial	**Labiodental**	**Interdental**	**Alveolar**	**Palatal**	**Velar**
Manner of production	**Oral stop** voiceless voiced	p (pin) b (bin)			t (tin) d (din)		k (kin) g (get)
	Nasal stop voiced	m (map)			n (nap)		ŋ (sing)
	Fricative voiceless voiced		f (fin) v (van)	θ (thin) ð (than)	s (sin) z (zone)	ʃ (shin) ʒ (leisure)	
	Affricate voiceless voiced					tʃ (chin) dʒ (gin)	
	Liquid voiced				l (law) r (raw)		
	Glides voiced					j (yes)	w (we)

Copyright © 1993 by Harcourt Brace & Company. All rights reserved.

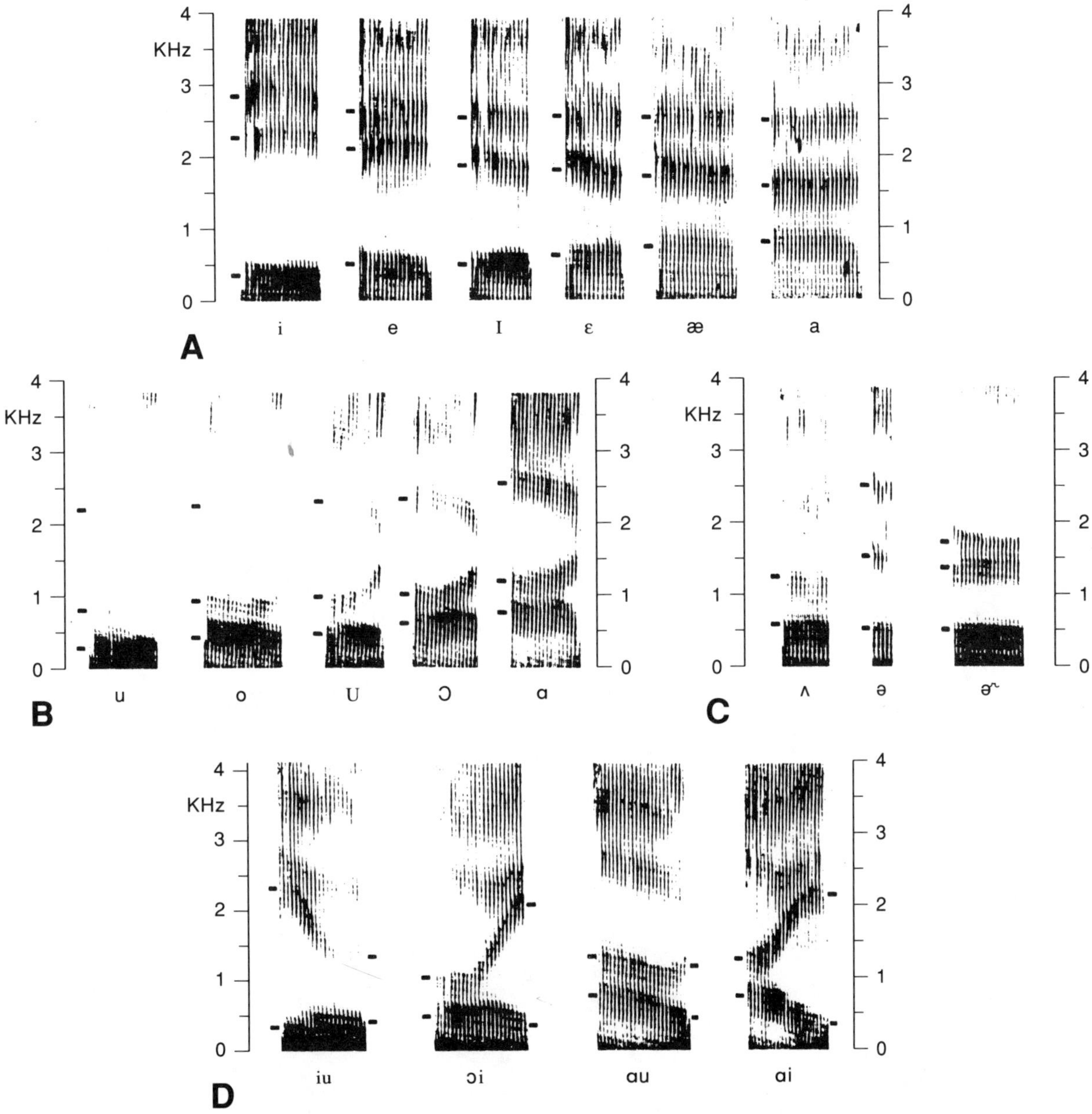

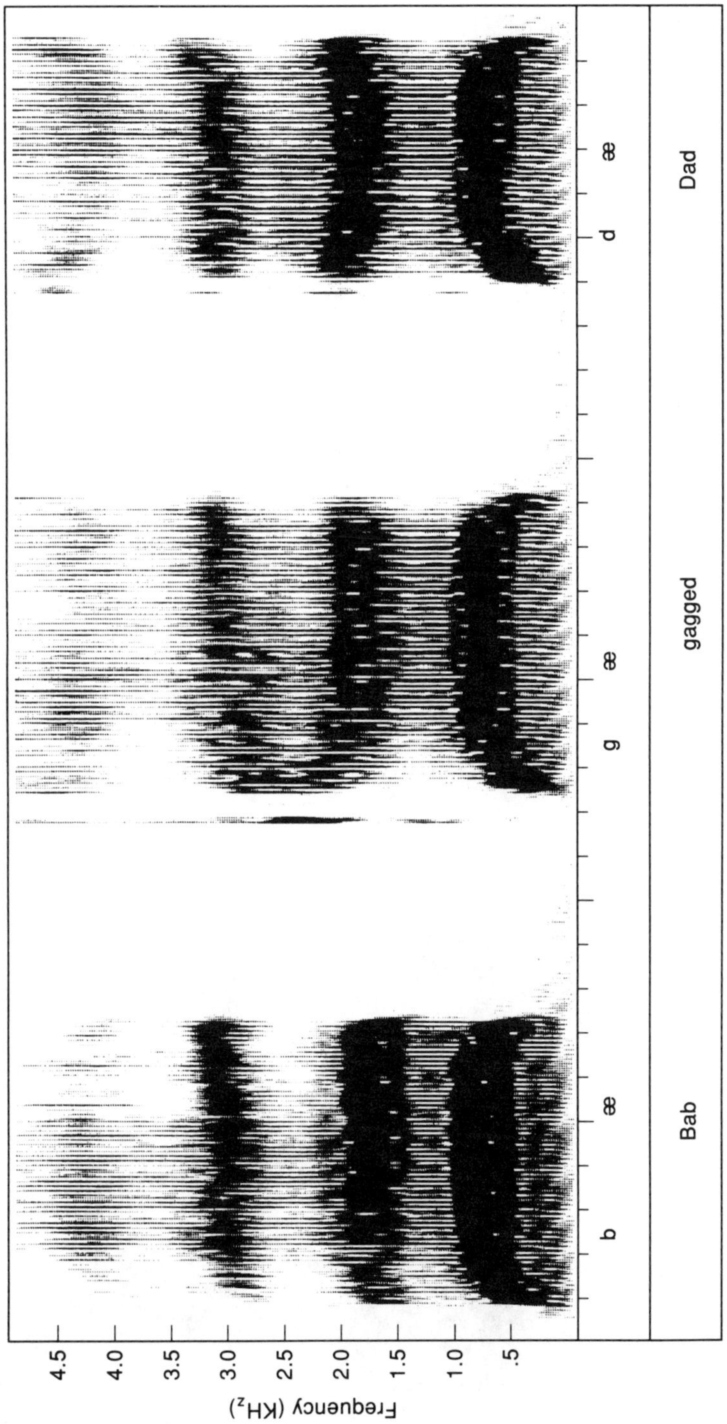
Frequency (KH$_z$)
4.5
4.0
3.5
3.0
2.5
2.0
1.5
1.0
.5
b
æ
Bab
g
æ
gagged
d
æ
Dad

di ti

Copyright © 1993 by Harcourt Brace & Company. All rights reserved.

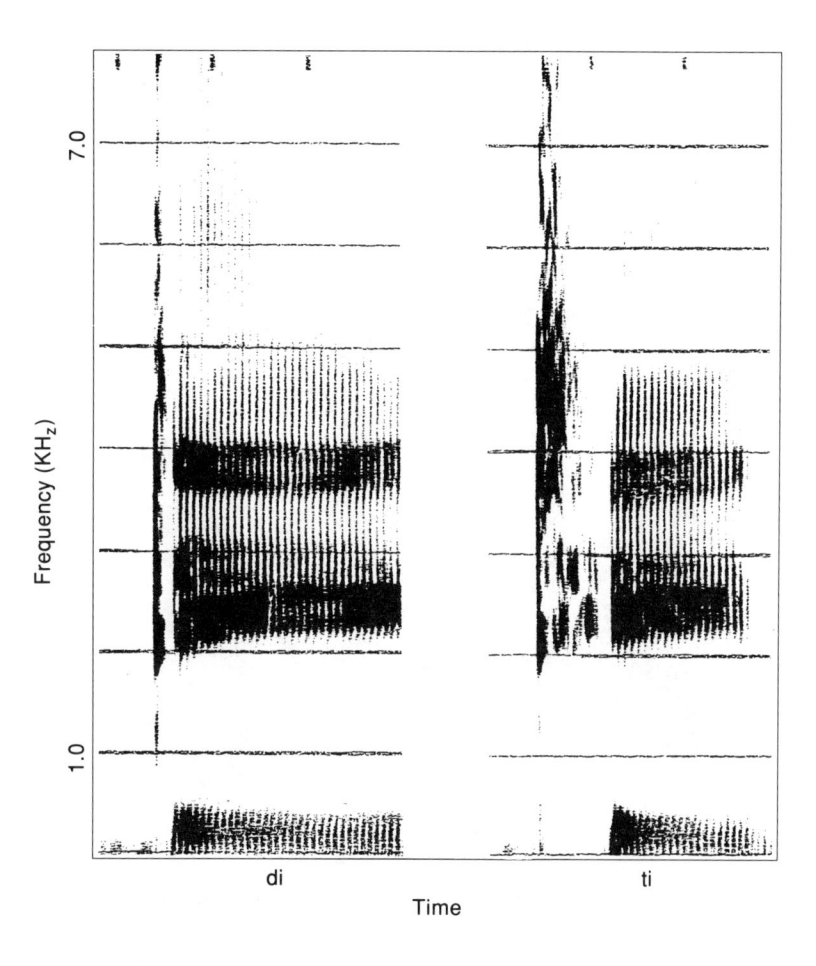

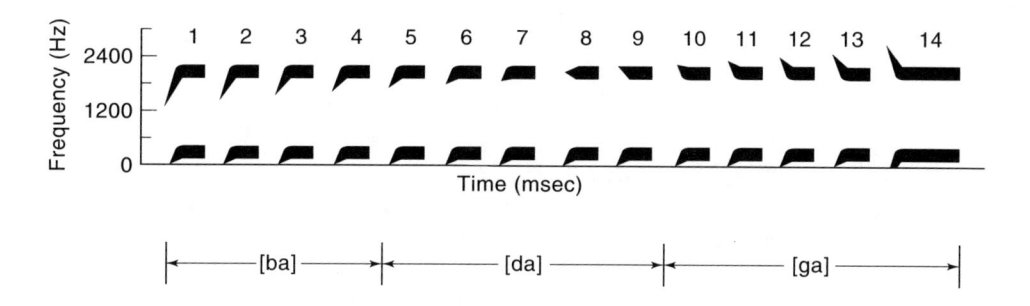

```
                          ┌─────────────┐
                          │  Cognitive  │
                          │   system    │
  The lexicon             └─────────────┘
┌─────────────────────────────────────────────────┐
│   ┌──────────┐    ┌──────────┐    ┌──────────┐  │
│   │  Visual  │    │ Auditory │    │  Output  │  │
│   │ logogens │    │ logogens │    │ logogens │  │
│   └──────────┘    └──────────┘    └──────────┘  │
└─────────────────────────────────────────────────┘
     ↑                  ↑                ↓
┌──────────┐       ┌──────────┐    ┌──────────┐
│  Visual  │       │ Auditory │    │ Response │
│ analysis │       │ analysis │    │  buffer  │
└──────────┘       └──────────┘    └──────────┘
     ↑                  ↑                ↓
```

Copyright © 1993 by Harcourt Brace & Company. All rights reserved.

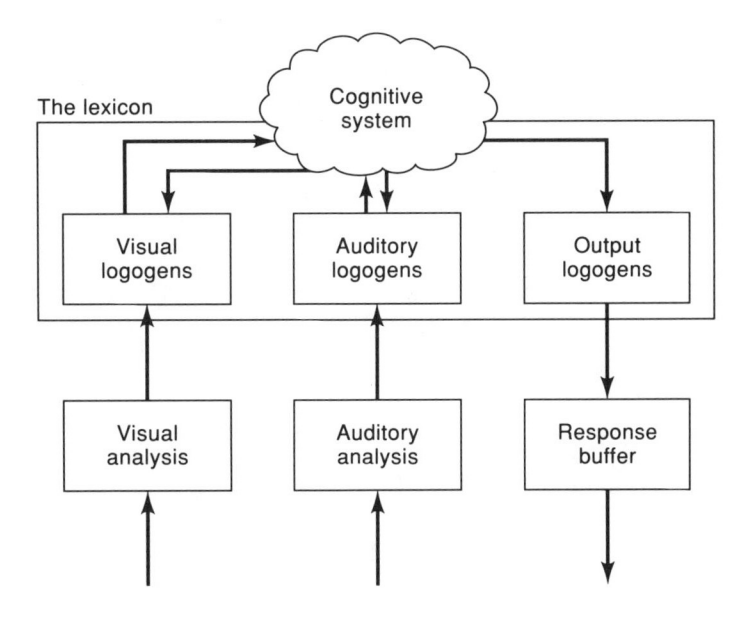

Copyright © 1993 by Harcourt Brace & Company. All rights reserved.

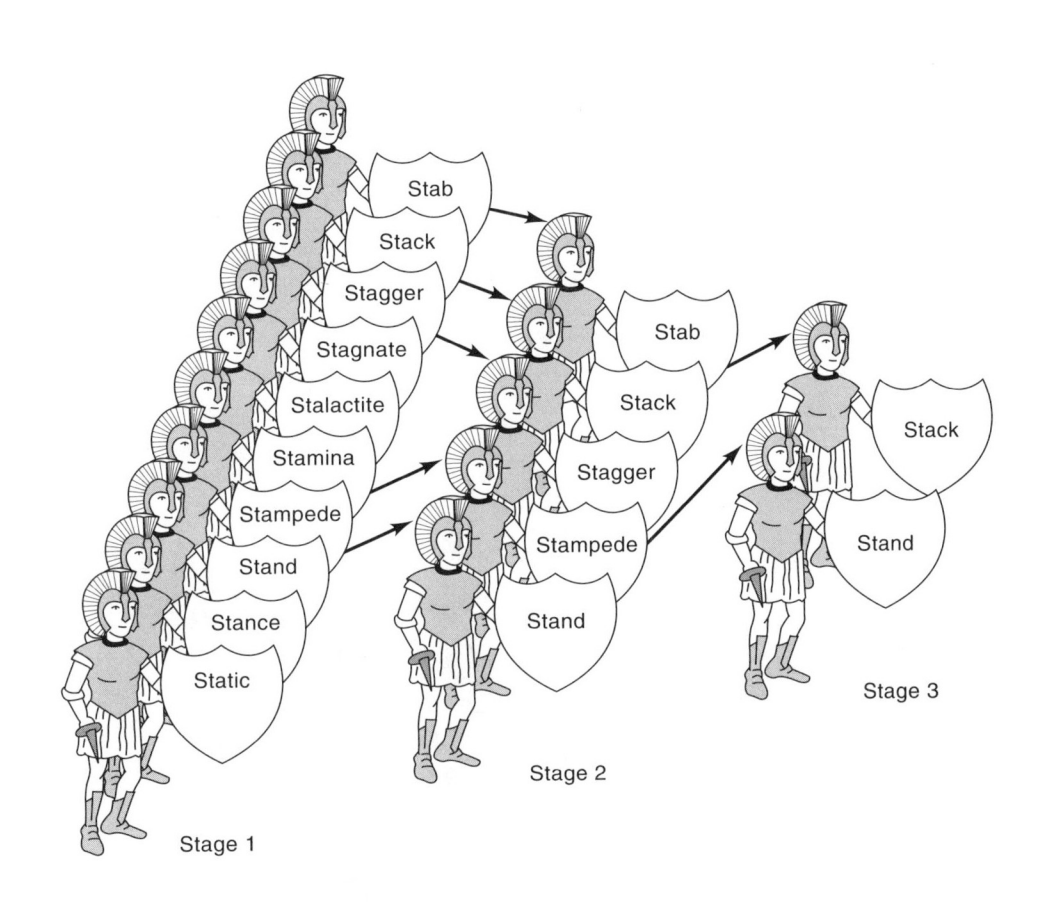

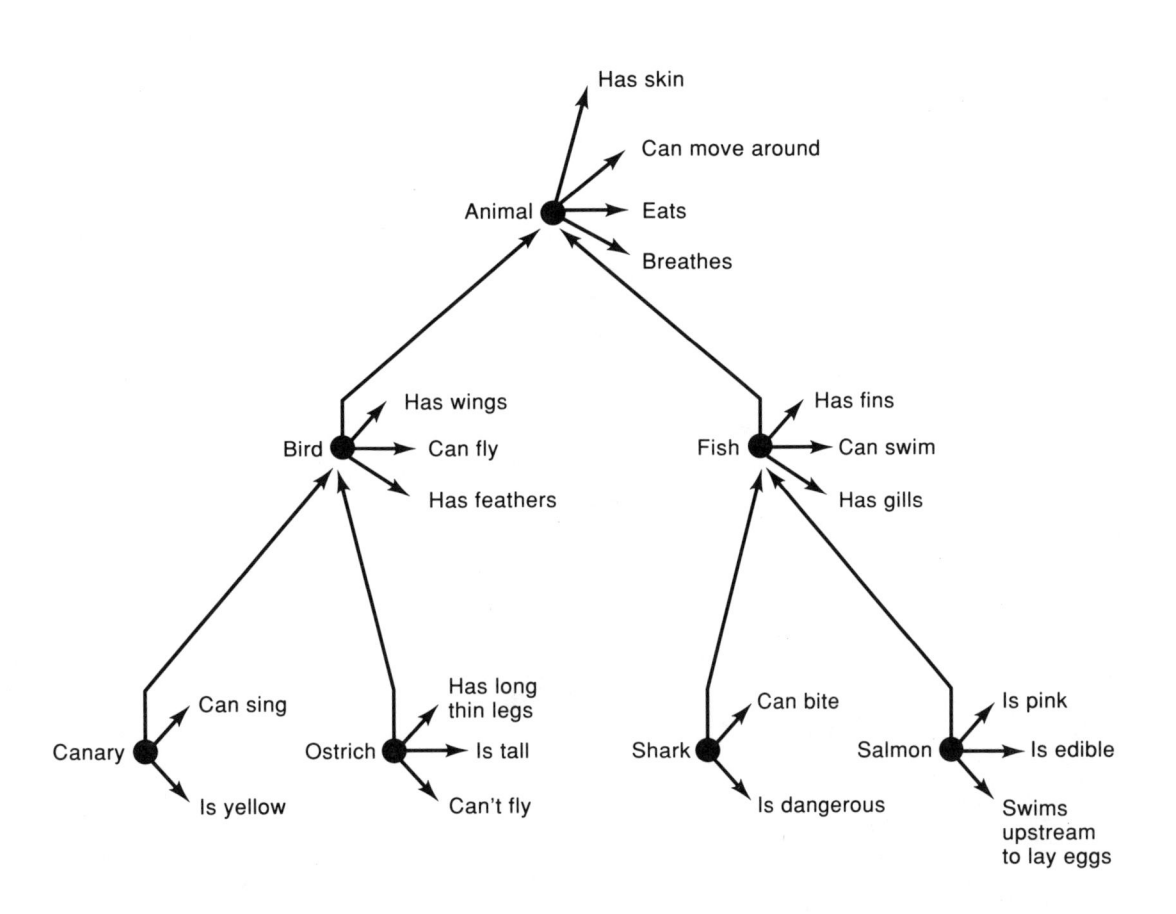

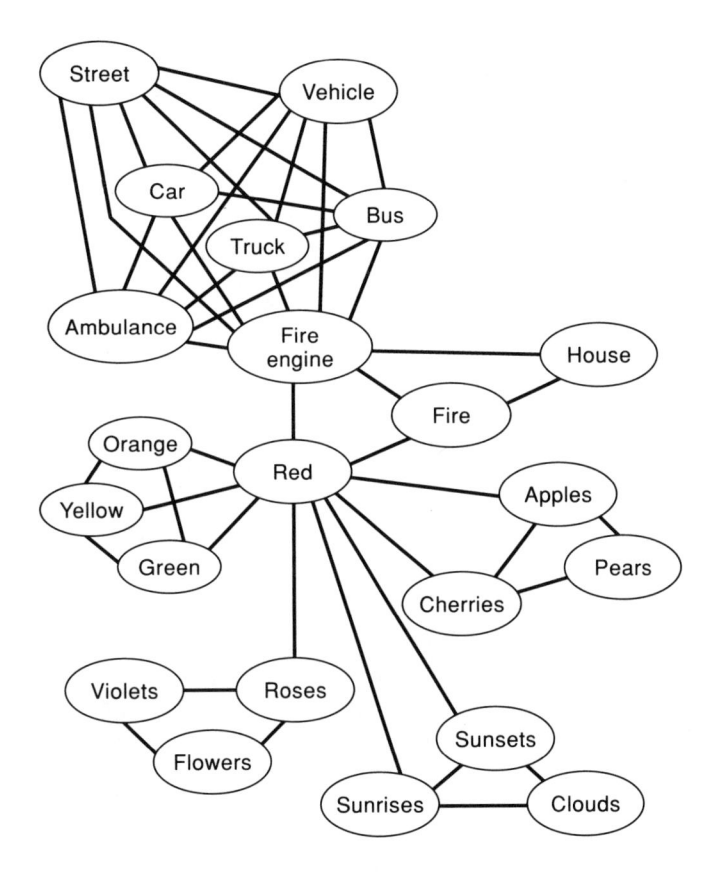

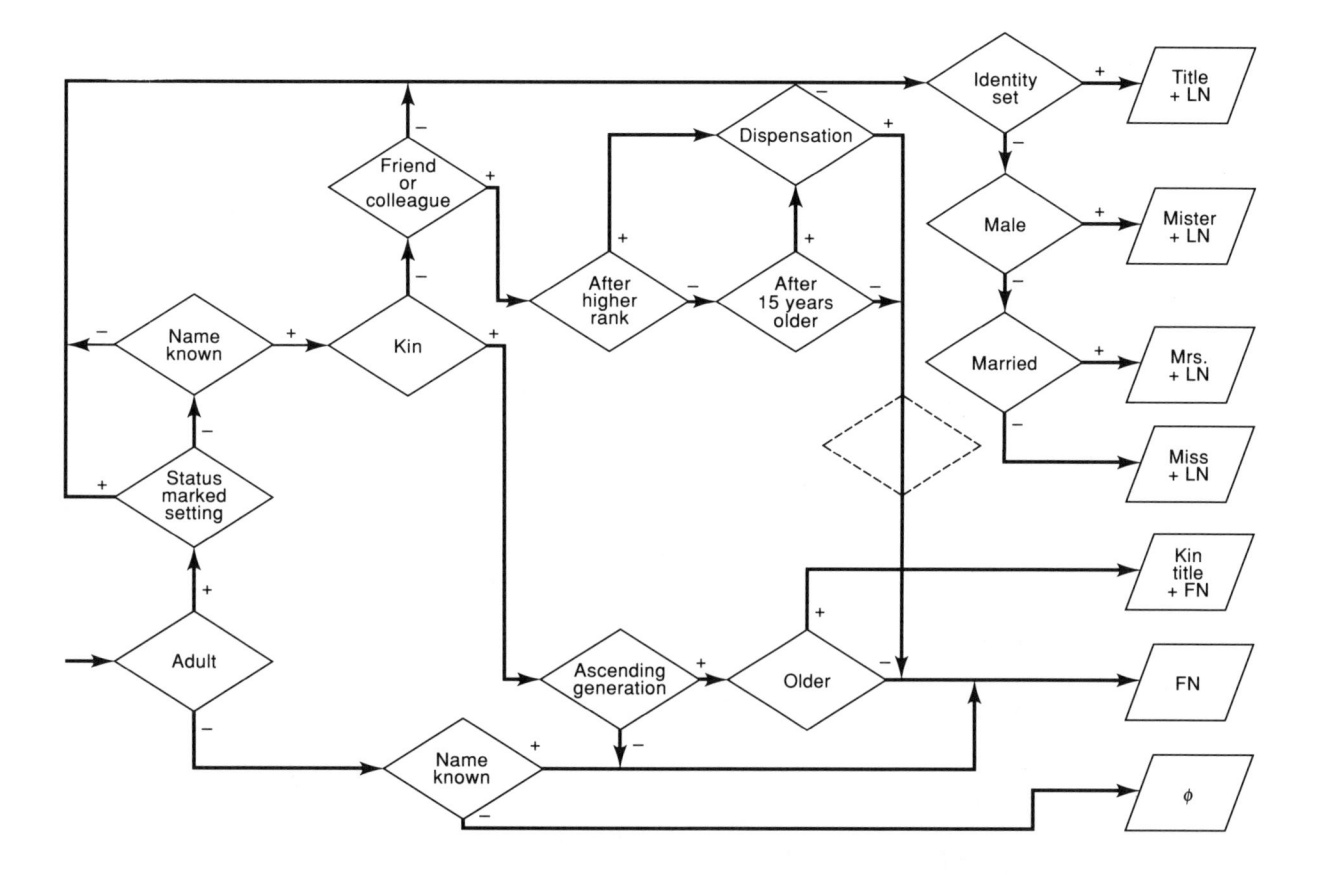

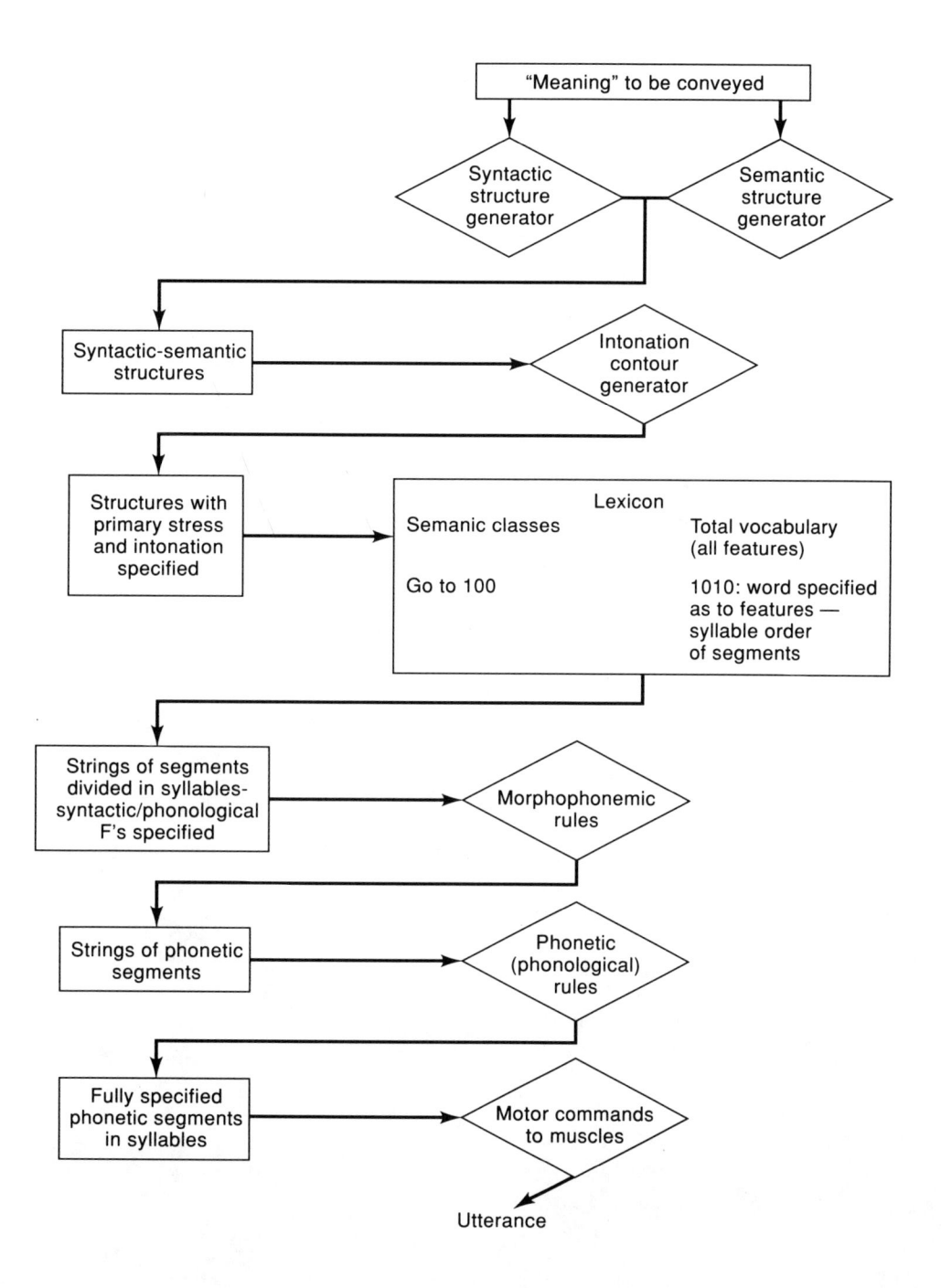

```
                    ┌─────────────────────┐
                    │ "Meaning" to be conveyed │
                    └─────────────────────┘
                       ↓              ↓
              ◇ Syntactic         ◇ Semantic
                structure           structure
                generator           generator

   ┌──────────────┐
   │ Syntactic-semantic │ ──→ ◇ Intonation
   │   structures       │       contour
   └──────────────┘             generator

   ┌──────────────┐         ┌──────────────────────────────────┐
   │ Structures with │      │              Lexicon              │
   │ primary stress  │ ──→  │ Semantic classes   Total vocabulary│
   │ and intonation  │      │                    (all features) │
   │   specified     │      │ Go to 100          1010: word specified│
   └──────────────┘         │                    as to features —│
                            │                    syllable order  │
                            │                    of segments     │
                            └──────────────────────────────────┘

   ┌──────────────┐
   │ Strings of segments │
   │ divided in syllables-│ ──→ ◇ Morphophonemic
   │ syntactic/phonological│      rules
   │ F's specified        │
   └──────────────┘

   ┌──────────────┐
   │ Strings of phonetic │ ──→ ◇ Phonetic
   │    segments          │      (phonological)
   └──────────────┘              rules

   ┌──────────────┐
   │ Fully specified │ ──→ ◇ Motor commands
   │ phonetic segments│      to muscles
   │  in syllables    │           ↓
   └──────────────┘          Utterance
```

Copyright © 1993 by Harcourt Brace & Company. All rights reserved.

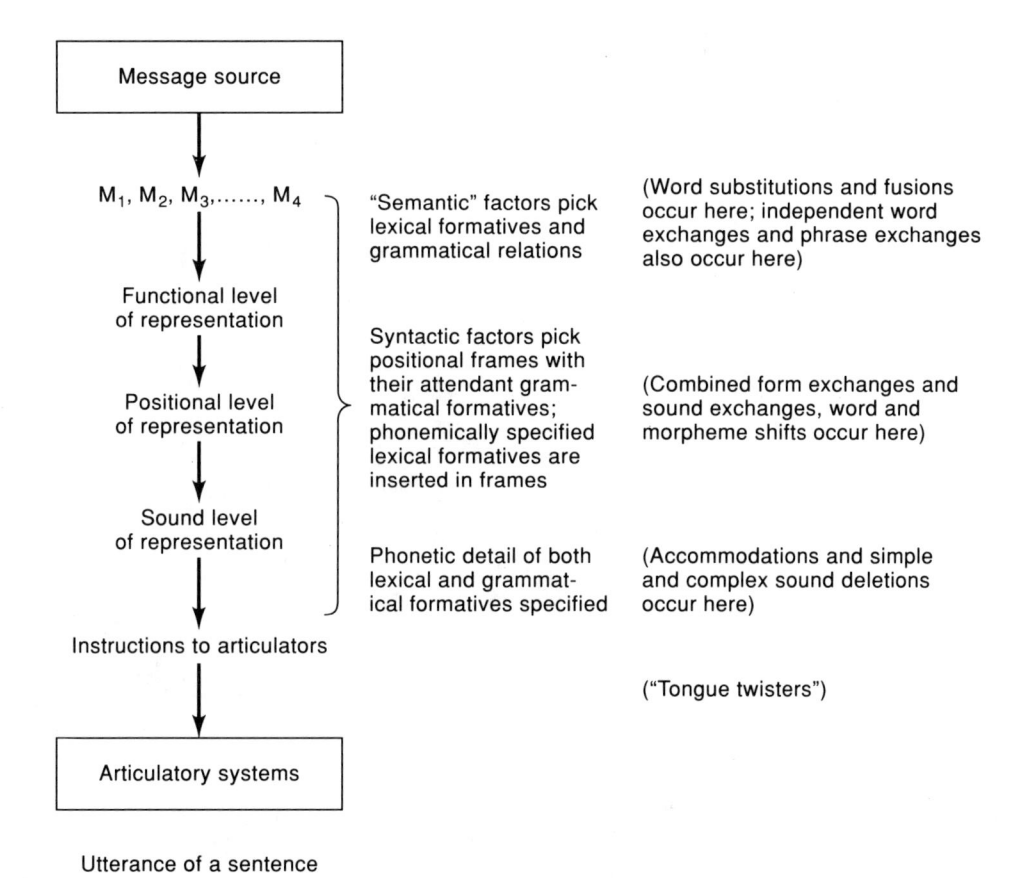

```
                ┌─────────────────┐
                │  Message source │
                └────────┬────────┘
                         ↓
         M₁, M₂, M₃,......, M₄  ⎫   "Semantic" factors pick      (Word substitutions and fusions
                         ↓      ⎪   lexical formatives and        occur here; independent word
                                ⎪   grammatical relations         exchanges and phrase exchanges
                Functional level⎪                                 also occur here)
                of representation⎪
                         ↓       ⎬  Syntactic factors pick
                                ⎪   positional frames with        (Combined form exchanges and
                Positional level⎪   their attendant gram-         sound exchanges, word and
                of representation⎪  matical formatives;           morpheme shifts occur here)
                         ↓      ⎪   phonemically specified
                                ⎪   lexical formatives are
                Sound level     ⎪   inserted in frames
                of representation⎪
                         ↓      ⎪   Phonetic detail of both       (Accommodations and simple
                                ⎪   lexical and grammat-          and complex sound deletions
              Instructions to   ⎭   ical formatives specified     occur here)
                articulators
                         ↓                                        ("Tongue twisters")
                ┌─────────────────┐
                │Articulatory     │
                │    systems      │
                └─────────────────┘

              Utterance of a sentence
```

Copyright © 1993 by Harcourt Brace & Company. All rights reserved.